WEST HAM UNITED
On This Day

WEST HAM UNITED
On This Day

History, Facts & Figures
from Every Day of the Year

JOHN NORTHCUTT

WEST HAM UNITED
On This Day

History, Facts & Figures from Every Day of the Year

All statistics, facts and figures are correct as of 1st August 2015

© John Northcutt

John Northcutt has asserted his rights in accordance with the Copyright, Designs and Patents Act 1988 to be identified as the author of this work.

Published By: Pitch Publishing Ltd, A2 Yeoman Gate, Durrington BN13 3QZ

Email: info@pitchpublishing.co.uk
Web: www.pitchpublishing.co.uk

First published 2008
Reprinted 2015

A catalogue record for this book is available from the British Library.

10-digit ISBN: 1-9054111-6-2
13-digit ISBN: 978-1-9054111-6-0

Printed and bound in India by Replika Press Pvt. Ltd.

FOREWORD BY TONY COTTEE

I loved my time at West Ham United and, of course, I still hold the club very close to my heart. It has always been a huge part of my life, and reading this super book has brought back many happy memories of my time as a Hammer.

My debut came on New Year's Day 1983 when we beat our London rivals Spurs 3-0. I was a fresh-faced 17-year-old striker and opened the scoring after 25 minutes and at the end of the game I was given the matchball to keep (although I didn't score a hat-trick). I still have that ball at home.

The 1985/86 season: that unforgettable campaign which saw West Ham run eventual champions Liverpool so close, as serious contenders for the title, obviously features heavily. A third-placed finish remains the club's best-ever top-flight season to this day.

In 1988 I moved to Everton, who paid a British record transfer fee of over £2m. But, on 17th September 1994, I made an emotional return to Upton Park, and several games from my second spell with the club also feature, as do many West Ham legends from throughout the club's history.

My old forward partner Frank McAvennie, and other former team-mates feature, such as: Trevor Brooking, Alvin Martin, Billy Bonds, and Julian Dicks. And, of course, those standout names from further back: Bobby Moore, Geoff Hurst, Martin Peters, Vic Watson, Jimmy Ruffell and Jim Barrett.

All the great games and memorable days are in here too, and its unique format means you can read it all in one go, or make it last all year, as you criss-cross through the club's history. John has produced a book which gives a great insight into the history of West Ham and it is a must for all Hammers fans.

Tony Cottee, West Ham United 1982-88, 1994-96

INTRODUCTION

It was in September 1959 as a schoolboy that I first saw a match at Upton Park, and for the record the Hammers beat West Bromwich Albion 4-1. That started for me on that afternoon some 49 years ago, a passion and fascination for the Hammers which has never waned.

During that time there have been many highs and lows, with the joy of winning the FA Cup and the gloom in being knocked out by a minor opponent. What great players I have been fortunate to see in action. In the sixties it was Johnny Byrne, Geoff Hurst, Bobby Moore and Martin Peters. Along came the seventies with Billy Bonds, Frank Lampard Senior and Pop Robson. The eighties gave us some exciting sides containing the likes of Alvin Martin, Phil Parkes, Alan Devonshire, Frank McAvennie and Tony Cottee. More recently we have been able to marvel at the skills of Joe Cole and Paolo Di Canio.

All these names and many more you will find in this book and I hope you enjoy reading about the activities of the club throughout the years. Some of you will be able to locate a match played on your date of birth and for others it will be an event on their birthday.

I would like to thank those at Pitch Publishing for giving me the opportunity to write this book and I am grateful to the production and editing team at Pitch who have done such a good job putting this book together. I am also indebted to three of my friends named below as each of their books proved invaluable in my research.

John Northcutt – September 2008

BIBLIOGRAPHY

West Ham United Miscellany, Brian Belton.
The Elite Era, A Complete Record, John Helliar.
Who's Who of West Ham United, Tony Hogg.

WEST HAM UNITED
On This Day

JANUARY

SATURDAY 1st JANUARY 1972

League leaders Manchester United were at Upton Park for a clash that attracted 41,892 fans. The game was a joy to watch as the Hammers midfield of Pop Robson, Trevor Brooking and Billy Bonds dominated. Robson opened the scoring just before half-time and further goals from Clyde Best and a Geoff Hurst penalty gave West Ham a deserved win. It was a great start to the New Year for the happy Hammers.

SATURDAY 1st JANUARY 1983

In a frenzied London derby against Tottenham, 17-year-old Tony Cottee made his league debut, scoring his first goal after 25 minutes. In the second half Devonshire was brought down and, from the resultant penalty, Ray Stewart puts the Hammers 2-0 up. To the delight of the majority of the 33,383 fans West Ham scored again ten minutes from time with a goal from Geoff Pike. Cottee was given the matchball.

SATURDAY 2nd JANUARY 1943

The 6,000 spectators at Upton Park for this wartime league game with Clapton Orient were treated to a goal fest. The Hammers beat their neighbours 10-3 with hat-tricks being scored by both Richard Dunn and George Foreman. Other scorers were Archie Macaulay and an own goal from Brooks while Sam Trigg, on loan from Birmingham, scored twice.

WEDNESDAY 2nd JANUARY 1974

Tomas Repka was born in Slavicin Zlin in the Czech Republic. An old-style full-back, he first joined Banik Ostrava – making 77 appearances – before signing for Sparta Prague in 1995. After 82 games he joined the Italian club Fiorentina in 1998 where he played 88 times in Serie A. He cost West Ham £5 million when they bought him in 2001. Tough in the tackle, he soon became a favourite of the Upton Park fans. Repka returned to his home country in 2006 after 164 league appearances.

FRIDAY 3rd JANUARY 1908

James Marshall was born in Stirlingshire. His first club was Glasgow Rangers, where he won six Scottish League Championship medals. He gained three Scotland caps – all against England. In 1934 he was transferred to Arsenal. He made four appearances in one season, before joining West Ham in 1935; he played 57 league games scoring 14 goals.

SATURDAY 3RD JANUARY 1931

West Ham were at home to Aston Villa, having lost 6-1 at Villa Park earlier that season. Villa centre-forward Tom Waring scored four goals that day. However, he was injured, but not missed as the Villa scored five. In an amazing match West Ham also scored five with goals from Viv Gibbins (two), Jimmy Harris, Tommy Yews and Jim Barrett.

SATURDAY 4TH JANUARY 1958

The third round of the FA Cup brought Blackpool and the famous Stanley Matthews to Upton Park. Second Division Hammers were not overawed by their First Division opponents. Hugh Kelly scored from the penalty spot to put Blackpool ahead after only two minutes. West Ham came back with a vengeance as Vic Keeble scored a hat-trick and a further two goals from Johnny Dick gave the Hammers a 5-1 victory.

SATURDAY 4TH JANUARY 1975

In the FA Cup at Southampton the Hammers raced into a 2-0 half-time lead. The goals came from a Frank Lampard free-kick and a header from Bobby Gould. Gould was later substituted after breaking his leg. The Saints reduced their deficit in the second half after Mick Channon scored a penalty following a foul on Stokes. The Hammers ran out 2-1 winners and went on to win the cup at Wembley.

FRIDAY 5TH JANUARY 1900

Billy Henderson was born on this day in January 1900 in Whitburn in County Durham. He joined West Ham in 1922 from the Welsh club Aberdare. A year later the full-back played in the first FA Cup Final at Wembley against Bolton. He played in 162 league games and a further 21 FA Cup ties. He only scored one goal which was, amazingly, against his old club Aberdare in the FA Cup. Tragically, in 1930, Billy died of tuberculosis aged 30.

SATURDAY 5TH JANUARY 1918

Playing in the London Combination during the First World War, the Hammers entertained their neighbours Clapton Orient. A crowd of 8,000 saw West Ham triumph 3-0 with goals from Frank Roberts (two) and the legendary Syd Puddefoot.

SATURDAY 5TH JANUARY 1991

Lowly Aldershot from the Fourth Division were drawn at home to West Ham in the third round of the FA Cup. To attract a bigger crowd the game was switched to Upton Park where an attendance of 22,929 saw the Shots gain a creditable 0-0 draw. Some 11 days later West Ham made up for their lapse by thrashing Aldershot 6-1 in the replay.

SATURDAY 6TH JANUARY 1940

Due to the outbreak of war the Football League fixtures were cancelled and West Ham played in the League South. On this day they were at home to Southend United. There were 5,200 fans to see the Hammers win 4-0 with a brace of goals from both Sammy Small and George Foreman.

WEDNESDAY 6TH JANUARY 1943

Ronnie Boyce was born in West Ham. He made his debut in a 5-2 win against Preston in 1960, he went on to play in a total of 282 league games, scoring 21 goals. Boyce was a midfield dynamo who never stopped running. His main claim to fame came in 1964 when he scored twice against Manchester United in the FA Cup semi-final and then went on to score the winning goal in the FA Cup Final against Preston North End.

SATURDAY 6TH JANUARY 2002

West Ham travelled to Macclesfield for an FA Cup third-round tie. The Cheshire side were captained by former Hammer Kevin Keen. There were 5,706 at the tiny Moss Rose ground to see future England stars Jermain Defoe (two) and Joe Cole score the goals in a 3-0 victory.

SATURDAY 7TH JANUARY 1984

Fourth Division Wigan were at Upton Park for a third-round FA Cup tie. They gave the Hammers a tough time, but lost to a penalty scored by Ray Stewart. It wasn't all good news: a bad injury to Alan Devonshire left him sidelined with torn ankle ligaments for 19 months.

SATURDAY 7TH JANUARY 1995

West Ham found themselves playing Wycombe Wanderers for the first time. The Hammers were in Buckinghamshire for the FA Cup third round. The tie attracted 9,007 spectators who saw West Ham win 2-0 with goals from Tony Cottee and substitute Kenny Brown.

SATURDAY 8TH JANUARY 1927

There were 44,417 spectators at Upton Park for the third round FA Cup tie with Tottenham. In an exciting London derby, Dimmock and Handley scored for Spurs but the Hammers won 3-2 with centre-forward Vic Watson grabbing a hat trick.

THURSDAY 8TH JANUARY 1953

Winger Johnny Ayris was born in Wapping, London. He made his debut against Burnley in October 1970 and went on to play in 57 league games and eight FA Cup ties. In 1971 he represented England Youth on seven occasions. He later played for Wimbledon and Brentford.

SATURDAY 8TH JANUARY 1989

In an exciting FA Cup tie at Upton Park the Hammers find themselves leading 2-0 against Arsenal after 41 minutes, courtesy of goals from Dickens and a Bould own-goal. Unfortunately the Gunners fought back to equalise with two goals from Paul Merson to see the game finish all-square. A goal from Rosenior ensured West Ham won the replay 1-0.

SATURDAY 9TH JANUARY 1965

Cup holders West Ham entertained Birmingham City in a third round FA Cup match at Upton Park. The Blues raced into a two goal lead but the Hammers were not giving up lightly as Johnny Byrne pulled a goal back just before half-time. Early in the second half, Geoff Hurst equalised and from then on there was only going to be one winner. Another goal from Hurst followed and Johnny Sissons grabbed a fourth.

SATURDAY 9TH JANUARY 1971

Paul Kitson was born in Durham. He signed for West Ham in February 1997, and his and John Hartson's goals helped save West Ham from relegation that season. He left after four seasons, and 18 goals (his last goals were a hat-trick against Charlton in November 2001). He later played for Brighton & Hove Albion and Rushden & Diamonds.

TUESDAY 9TH JANUARY 1979

A crowd of 14,124 saw an upset at Somerton Park as Fourth Division Newport County took on the Hammers in the FA Cup. The Welshmen won 2-1, scoring their winner nine minutes from time.

THURSDAY 10TH JANUARY 1918

Inside-forward Les Bennett was born in Wood Green, north London. He made 273 league appearances for Tottenham before joining West Ham in 1954. He made his debut against Derby County on Christmas Day 1954 and went on to make 47 appearances, scoring three goals. He later played in non-league football for both Clacton and Romford.

SATURDAY 10TH JANUARY 1942

In a wartime London League match at Aldershot the Hammers triumphed 5-1. Goalscorers were Quickenden, Foreman and a treble from Eddie Chapman. The hat-trick hero went on to become the club secretary where he went on to give the club 49 years' service.

SATURDAY 10TH JANUARY 1987

The Hammers are away to neighbours Orient in the third round of the FA Cup. Centre-half Paul Hilton puts West Ham ahead in the first half but, just as they were heading to the next round, the Orient equalised thanks to a last-minute penalty from Castle. The Hammers won the replay 4-1.

SATURDAY 11TH JANUARY 1930

Centre-forward Vic Watson continued his amazing scoring record by grabbing two more against Notts County in the FA Cup third round. Further goals from Jim Barrett and Viv Gibbins in the 4-0 victory sent the Upton Park crowd home happy.

SATURDAY 11TH JANUARY 1936

There was a huge crowd of 42,000 at Upton Park for the FA Cup third round match with Luton Town. Dave Mangnall and Jimmy Ruffell were the West Ham scorers in an exciting 2-2 draw. In the replay, the Hammers were well beaten – losing 4-0.

TUESDAY 11TH JANUARY 1955

Born on this day in Liverpool was centre-half Joe Gallagher. He started his career at Birmingham City then went on to play for Wolves. Joe joined West Ham in 1982 and made 11 appearances for the club before going on to play with Burnley, who were managed by former Hammer John Bond.

SATURDAY 12TH JANUARY 1924

A third round FA Cup tie at Upton Park with Third Division Aberdare Athletic as the visitors. The Hammers – who were beaten finalists the previous season – were on top throughout and ran out 5-0 winners. Billy Brown scored twice with further goals coming from Henderson, Moore and Williams.

THURSDAY 12TH JANUARY 1967

Future Hammer Marco Boogers was born in Dordrecht, Holland. After scoring 103 goals for five different Dutch clubs there was a cause for optimism when the striker joined West Ham in 1995 for £1 million. However, he turned out to be possibly one of the worst signings in the club's history! After being sent off at Old Trafford in only his second match, he managed to feature in just two others before he was sent packing back to Holland where he joined Volendam.

SATURDAY 12TH JANUARY 1974

The eagerly-awaited clash with Manchester United took place at Upton Park. Billy Bonds put the Hammers in the lead just after half-time but McIlroy equalised. Then, with seven minutes remaining, Pat Holland scored with a header which delighted the majority of the 34,147 crowd. This win prompted West Ham to go on an unbeaten nine-match run.

SATURDAY 13TH JANUARY 1906

Southern League side West Ham were drawn away to play the mighty Woolwich Arsenal at Plumstead. Before a sizeable 18,000 crowd, the Hammers did well in gaining a 1-1 draw. The Hammers' goal was scored from a penalty taken by goalkeeper George Kitchen. West Ham lost the replay 2-3.

SATURDAY 13TH JANUARY 1923

West Ham kicked off their 1923 FA Cup campaign with the long trip north to Hull City. A crowd of around 14,000 spectators saw legendary centre-forward Vic Watson score twice, and a further goal from Billy Moore gave the Hammers a 3-2 victory. It was the start of an historic cup run, as later that season West Ham went on to play in the first FA Cup Final to be held at Wembley.

SUNDAY 14TH JANUARY 1968

Winger Marc Keller was born in Colmar, France. He started out in the French league with Mulhouse before joining Strasbourg in 1990. He later gained international recognition and scored against England in 1997. Moving on to Karlsruhe, in Germany, he scored 13 times in two seasons for them. Manager Harry Redknapp bought him in 1998 where he made 57 appearances for the Hammers, scoring six goals. He later joined Blackburn on a free transfer where he made five appearances before returning home to become a director at Strasbourg.

SATURDAY 14TH JANUARY 1989

Lying 20th in the table, this was a vital win for West Ham at the Baseball Ground. After only a minute they were losing 1-0 to Derby County but goals from David Kelly and Liam Brady gave the East Londoners a welcome three points.

SATURDAY 14TH JANUARY 1995

A home London derby against rivals Tottenham saw the Hammers gain an early lead with a headed goal from Jerome Boere. However, the home faithful among the crowd of 24,573 were left rueing Teddy Sheringham and Jurgen Klinsman goals which gave Spurs a 2-1 win.

THURSDAY 15TH JANUARY 1920

In the season where West Ham became a member of the Football League they were at home in an FA Cup replay against Southampton. There were 25,000 gathered to see Syd Puddefoot score twice with a further goal from George Butcher during a 3-1 win.

SATURDAY 15TH JANUARY 1966

Northampton Town were the visitors to Upton Park for a First Division fixture. The Cobblers were languishing at the bottom of the league but took the lead after 14 minutes. A penalty scored by Geoff Hurst in the second half levelled the score, which remained 1-1 to the end.

SATURDAY 16TH JANUARY 1932

The Hammers were looking for three successive wins when they travelled to Middlesbrough. Despite Vic Watson scoring twice they still lost the game 3-2. At the end of that season, West Ham were relegated.

JEROME BOERE

FRIDAY 16TH JANUARY 1981

Bobby Zamora was born in Barking, Essex. He started his career at Bristol Rovers, where he made six sub appearances. A fee of £100,000 took him to Brighton & Hove Albion in 2000 where he was successful in scoring 76 league goals, before joining Spurs in 2003. He only managed one goal for them before arriving at West Ham in 2004 as part of a swap deal involving Jermain Defoe – and his goal against Preston North End in the Play-Off Final in 2005 ensured West Ham returned to the Premiership. He left West Ham for Fulham in July 2008.

SATURDAY 16TH JANUARY 1982

Making his debut at the Goldstone Ground, the home of Brighton, was Francois Van Der Elst. He came on as a second half substitute to no avail as the Seagulls ran out 1-0 winners before 22,591 spectators. The Belgian Van Der Elst went on to make 70 appearances for the club.

SATURDAY 17TH JANUARY 1942

In a wartime league game at The Den, West Ham were looking to do the double over Millwall, and in front of 4,000 fans the Hammers did just that. West Ham were worthy 3-1 winners in the London derby – with goals coming from Sam Small, Eddie Chapman and Stan Foxall.

THURSDAY 17TH JANUARY 1946

Born on this day in Leigh-on-Sea was Martin Britt. He came to fame at West Ham when facing Liverpool in the 1963 FA Youth Cup Final. The Hammers were trailing 4-1 in the second-leg when he amazingly scored four headed goals to ensure that West Ham won the cup. He went on to make 26 first-team appearances before joining Blackburn Rovers in 1965. After only six outings for them his career ended through injury.

SATURDAY 17TH JANUARY 1981

It was top versus third in the the old Second Division, as leaders West Ham were away at third-placed Notts County. A crowd of 13,745 witnessed the 1-1 draw. Pat Holland scored the Hammers' goal – but it was costly as he injured his knee as he scored and as a result did not play again that season. Nonetheless West Ham won the league, while County finished second.

SATURDAY 18TH JANUARY 1913

West Ham were enjoying a good season in the Southern League, so it came as a shock when they travelled to Merthyr Town and lost 6-2. The Hammers' two goals were scored by George Butcher in front of some 4,000 fans.

SATURDAY 18TH JANUARY 1992

It was a top-flight basement battle, as the First Division's two bottom teams swapped places in the drop zone after the Hammers won 1-0 at Luton Town. Substitute Mike Small – signed from Brighton for £400,000 at the start of the 1991/92 season – was the goalscorer in the second half with 11,088 in attendance.

THURSDAY 18TH JANUARY 2001

Popular central defender Javier Margas returns to Chile as he is forced to retire due to knee problems. To show his commitment to the club he often dyed his hair claret & blue. He had played in a total of 22 league games, scoring one goal.

SATURDAY 19TH JANUARY 1901

After changing their name from Thames Ironworks this season the team were known as West Ham United. By beating Swindon Town at home they achieved the double over the Wiltshire team. Four thousand fans saw the Hammers win 3-1 with goals from Fred Corbett (two) and Billy Grassam.

SATURDAY 19TH JANUARY 1957

West Ham recorded their seventh consecutive home league win by beating Port Vale 2-1 at Upton Park. A crowd of 17,229 were in attendance to see Scotsman Johnny Dick and John Smith get the Hammers' goals that afternoon.

SATURDAY 19TH JANUARY 1991

In beating Leicester City at Upton Park West Ham recorded their third consecutive 1-0 win in the old Second Division. There was a crowd of 21,652 present to see George Parris score the only goal of the game, and the win kept leaders West Ham five points ahead of second-placed Oldham Athletic in the race for promotion.

SATURDAY 20TH JANUARY 1900

Playing their last season as Thames Ironworks, the club travelled to Kent to play Sheppey United in the Southern League. Prior to this match, the Ironworks had gone seven games without a win. It was pleasing, therefore, to record a 3-0 win with goals from Carnelly, Joyce and McKay.

SATURDAY 20TH JANUARY 1979

Going for promotion from the Second Division, the Hammers arrive at Bristol Rovers in fourth place. Trevor Brooking showed his silky skills to those 12,418 present and it was Pop Robson who scored the only goal of the game for West Ham.

TUESDAY 20TH JANUARY 2004

The Hammers swooped to sign the Wimbledon duo Nigel Reo-Coker and Adam Nowland. England under-21 midfielder Reo-Coker was signed for a fee of £575,000 and later captained West Ham, before moving to Aston Villa for £7.5m. Nowland, also a central midfielder, cost half a million less at £75,000.

SATURDAY 21ST JANUARY 1933

Without an away win all season it was just as well that the Hammers were doing well at home. On this occasion they were at home to Port Vale in a Second Division fixture which attracted a crowd of 13,908. West Ham won the game 5-0 with the goals coming from Vic Watson (two), Arthur Wilson (two) and Jim Barrett.

SATURDAY 21ST JANUARY 1967

West Ham entertained Sheffield Wednesday at Upton Park watched by 29,220 fans. With 25 minutes remaining the score was 0-0 and the crowd were restless. Then the goals came as Brian Dear, Geoff Hurst and Johnny Sissons scored in a convincing win.

MONDAY 22ND JANUARY 1900

Goalkeeper Alex Kane was born in Aberdeen. He began his career at Hearts before joining Reading in 1922 and then Portsmouth in 1923. After joining West Ham in 1926, he only played in two league games; both at home and both 2-1 defeats.

SATURDAY 22ND JANUARY 1972

The 31,045 fans at Upton Park were treated to a feast of goals in the clash with Derby County. It was 1-1 at half-time – Frank Lampard senior scored for the Hammers. West Ham twice took the lead in the second half, through Trevor Brooking and Pop Robson, only for Derby to equalise twice as the match ended 3-3.

WEDNESDAY 22ND JANUARY 2003

Not a good day at The Valley as Charlton beat West Ham 4-2. Worse was the fact that the two goals the Hammers scored were own-goals by Charlton players Richard Rufus and Mark Fish.

SATURDAY 23RD JANUARY 1943

A wartime league game at Upton Park which would have pleased the 8,000 fans present. Visitors Aldershot were beaten 6-3 with inside-forward Richard Dunn claiming a hat-trick.

SATURDAY 23RD JANUARY 1965

A cracking league game at Upton Park against Burnley ended 3-2. 25,490 spectators saw John Bond, Ron Boyce and Johnny Byrne score the West Ham goals.

TUESDAY 23RD JANUARY 2001

On loan striker Jermain Defoe scored for Bournemouth in their 2-0 win at Cambridge United. This event broke the Cherries' club record as Defoe had now scored in ten successive league games.

SATURDAY 24TH JANUARY 1987

The Hammers faced a trip to Coventry City for a First Division fixture. There were 14,170 spectators in attendance to see Tony Cottee score all three during a 3-1 win. This was the fourth consecutive season that West Ham had done the double over the Sky Blues.

WEDNESDAY 24TH JANUARY 1990

Midfielder Ralph Milne, who was on loan from Manchester United, made his debut in the League Cup at Derby County. The team were stricken with injuries but gave a battling performance to draw 0-0. The Hammers won the replay to move into the semi-final.

MONDAY 24th JANUARY 1994

A thriller at Upton Park as West Ham drew 3-3 with Norwich City. Sutton put the Canaries ahead but then equalised for West Ham with an own-goal. In the second half Steve Jones put West Ham in front but Norwich came back with two goals and were leading 3-2 with six minutes remaining. Trevor Morley then came on as substitute and promptly equalised to send the majority of the 20,738 fans home content.

SATURDAY 25th JANUARY 1902

Not having won for three games, the Hammers were keen to get back to winning ways when they travelled to Luton Town in the Southern League – and a crowd of approximately 5,000 fans saw them win 3-0 in convincing fashion. Fergus Hunt (two) and Billy Grassam were the scorers. This game was the start of an unbeaten run to the end of the season which saw the team finish in fourth place.

SATURDAY 25th JANUARY 1930

A fourth round FA Cup tie with Leeds United drew a huge 34,000 crowd to Upton Park. Centre-forward Vic Watson was having an amazing season, scoring plenty of goals. In the league he had already scored five goals against Leeds in the home and away encounters and, in this match, he scored a further four in the Hammers' 4-1 victory, taking his season's tally against the Yorkshire club alone to nine goals!

MONDAY 26th JANUARY 1931

There were only 9,090 in attendance for the home game with Newcastle United. Both teams were struggling near the bottom of the league but it was the Hammers who came out on top, winning 3-2. West Ham's three goals that day were scored by Wilf James, Viv Gibbins and Stan Earle, to ease relegation fears in east London.

SATURDAY 26th JANUARY 2002

FA Cup Fourth round day and West Ham played Chelsea at Stamford Bridge. Having lost there 5-1 only six days earlier in the Premier League, it was a much better performance this time as Fredi Kanoute scored in the 1-1 draw. However, the Blues triumphed in the replay at Upton Park on 6th February, winning 3-2 with a last-minute goal from defender John Terry.

SATURDAY 27TH JANUARY 1973

An amazing season for Pop Robson who was scoring plenty of goals. The London derby with Chelsea attracted 33,336 to the Boleyn ground. Tommy Taylor put West Ham ahead and two more goals from Robson saw West Ham win 3-1. It was the eighth time that Robson had scored twice in a match.

THURSDAY 27TH JANUARY 2005

Midfielders Gavin Williams and Carl Fletcher were named in the Welsh squad for a friendly with Hungary at the Millennium Stadium in Cardiff.

SATURDAY 27TH JANUARY 2007

Full-back Lucas Neill made his first-team debut in the FA Cup fourth-round tie with Watford at Upton Park, having signed from Blackburn Rovers in a £1.5m move. However, it was an unhappy debut as he limped off injured early in the second half. The game was poor and the unhappy Hammers lost 1-0 in front of 31,168 spectators, leaving them dumped out of the FA Cup.

SATURDAY 28TH JANUARY 1899

Having won every home game Thames Ironworks were confident of beating Chesham in this home Southern League match. They did in fact win handsomely, 8-1, with the goals coming from Gresham (two), Reynolds (two), Dove, Lloyd, McEachrane and Reid. That season Thames finished as Southern League Division Two champions.

SATURDAY 28TH JANUARY 1984

There were 27,590 present at Selhurst Park to see the fourth round FA Cup tie against Crystal Palace. The home side took the lead but a late West Ham equaliser came when Brooking set up Dave Swindlehurst. The Hammers won the replay 2-0.

SUNDAY 28TH JANUARY 2001

A never-to-be-forgotten day which saw West Ham dump the mighty Manchester United out of the FA Cup at Old Trafford. A second-half goal from Italian striker Paolo Di Canio did the damage. The goal was enough to send the 9,000 travelling Hammers' fans home jubilant and West Ham into the fifth round of that season's FA Cup.

FRIDAY 29TH JANUARY 1897

Barking, in Essex, was the birthplace of goalscorer Frank Richardson. He first joined Plymouth Argyle in 1921 – scoring 37 goals before coming to West Ham in 1923. With the Hammers he only scored twice in ten league games before leaving to play for Swindon Town in 1924. He scored 33 goals in 53 league games for the Wiltshire club and then joined Reading where his scoring record continued with another 44 goals in 91 matches.

SATURDAY 29TH JANUARY 1921

West Ham were enjoying their second season as a League club when they travelled to play Leeds United. Before a crowd of 15,000 at Elland Road it was the Hammers who won 2-1. The two goalscorers were centre-forward Syd Puddefoot and outside right George Carter.

SATURDAY 30TH JANUARY 1926

For the visit of Leeds United, centre-half Jim Barrett was moved to the forward line in place of the injured Earle. Big Jim revelled in his new role and scored a hat-trick in front of the Boleyn faithful. The game ended 4-2 with the other Hammers' goal coming from Billy Moore.

SATURDAY 30TH JANUARY 1982

The Hammers had not scored for three games coming into the home game with West Bromwich Albion. To the delight of the 24,423 fans West Ham won the game 3-1. There were two goals for centre-forward David Cross and one from fellow striker Paul Goddard.

SATURDAY 31ST JANUARY 1942

After four straight wins, West Ham were confident going into this game at Queens Park Rangers in the wartime league. On this occasion they slipped up, losing 2-1. Sammy Small got West Ham's goal.

SATURDAY 31ST JANUARY 1976

Paulo Wanchope was born in Costa Rica. He came to England in 1997 to play for Derby County where he scored 28 times in 83 appearances for the Rams. West Ham paid £3.5 million for his services in 1999: in one season he played 45 times, scoring 15 goals. Brilliant but erratic, Wanchope later played for Manchester City and Spanish club Malaga.

WEST HAM UNITED
On This Day

FEBRUARY

SATURDAY 1st FEBRUARY 1975

Carlisle United were making their first-ever visit to Upton Park for a league game. There were 26,805 in the ground to see West Ham win 2-0. Both goals came in the first half – from Billy Jennings and Pat Holland.

WEDNESDAY 1st FEBRUARY 1989

An FA Cup fourth round replay with Swindon Town attracts 24,723 fans to Upton Park. The Hammers progressed to round five after Leroy Rosenior scored the only goal of the game.

THURSDAY 1st FEBRUARY 1996

Manager Harry Redknapp signs the Portuguese international striker Dani on loan from Sporting Lisbon. He soon became a hero after scoring the winning goal against London rivals Tottenham. He scored a further goal that season in his nine appearances before returning to his home country.

SATURDAY 2nd FEBRUARY 1918

The day of a wartime home league game with London rivals Brentford. In an earlier encounter in the season the Hammers had beaten the Bees 8-3. The 5,000 crowd anticipated lots of goals and this was what they got as West Ham easily won 7-2. There were six different scorers; Bill Kirsopp (two), Herbert Ashton, Frank Roberts, Syd Puddefoot, Jack Mackesy and an own-goal.

SATURDAY 2nd FEBRUARY 1957

West Ham did the double over Barnsley by winning 2-1 at Oakwell. The 15,931 crowd saw goals from Johnny Dick and Billy Dare give the Londoners victory. It was the same pair who had scored in the earlier league game between the sides.

SATURDAY 3rd FEBRUARY 1996

A goal from Robbie Slater after 19 minutes was sufficient to earn West Ham all three points in a home Premiership game against Nottingham Forest. The Hammers were unlucky not to win by more, after a stunning speculative shot from the half-way line by Dani went narrowly wide.

SATURDAY 3rd FEBRUARY 2001

West Ham travelled to Anfield to play Liverpool in a Premiership fixture. Historically, Anfield has never been a happy hunting ground for the Hammers and on this occasion they duly lost again – 3-0.

TUESDAY 3rd FEBRUARY 2004

A double signing as midfielder Jobi McAnuff arrives from Wimbledon for £300,000 and coming on loan from Monaco was Seb Carole. McAnuff played a more prominent part at Upton Park, making 14 league appearances, whereas Carole only made one sub appearance.

SATURDAY 4th FEBRUARY 1911

The Southern League Hammers entertained First Division Preston North End in the FA Cup, and a big crowd of 12,000 saw George Webb score a hat-trick in a sensational 3-0 victory.

SATURDAY 4th FEBRUARY 1967

The visit of West Ham to Southampton attracted the south-coast side's biggest crowd for 18 years. A huge crowd of 30,123 flocked to The Dell for their First Division fixture. West Ham were overwhelmed in the first half and at the interval were losing 4-0. In the second half the Hammers reduced the deficit with goals from Jack Burkett and Geoff Hurst. However, the in-form Saints also scored two further goals and the game ended with West Ham losing 6-2.

SUNDAY 4th FEBRUARY 1996

A sad day. It was announced that Alan Sealey had died. He was the West Ham hero in the European Cup Winners' Cup Final against Munich in 1965, scoring both goals in the 2-0 win over TSV 1860 München. He played for the club from 1961 until 1967, scoring 22 goals in 107 league appearances. He later played for Plymouth Argyle and Romford.

SATURDAY 5th FEBRUARY 1944

A wartime league game with Southampton drew a crowd of 7,500 to Upton Park. It turned out to be an easy 4-1 win for the Hammers. George Foreman scored twice with further goals from Len Goulden and Maurice Dunkley – a guest player from Manchester City.

SATURDAY 5TH FEBRUARY 1955

Lowly Plymouth Argyle were swept away in this Second Division fixture at Upton Park. The 18,154 fans saw Dave Sexton score a fine hat-trick with further goals from Johnny Dick (two) and Les Bennett.

SATURDAY 5TH FEBRUARY 1966

It was a tough Division One encounter at fourth-placed Leeds with West Ham trailing 2-0 at half-time. By full-time the Hammers found themselves on the wrong end of a 5-0 scoreline. However, they then went on to win their next four games, scoring 14 goals in the process!

SATURDAY 6TH FEBRUARY 1971

West Ham played Derby County in the First Division at Upton Park. The main talking point was that Bobby Moore had been named as substitute. The Rams were in good form and were leading 3-0 at half-time. Bobby Moore came on in the second half and almost immediately Peter Eustace pulled a goal back but the game ended in a 4-1 defeat.

THURSDAY 6TH FEBRUARY 1986

West Ham were going well in the First Division in 1985/86, but league ambitions were put on hold on this snowy Tuesday evening, as the Hammers focused on an FA Cup fourth round second replay against Ipswich Town at Portman Road. A snow-covered pitch meant a red ball had to be used, and for much of the match it looked like another replay would be needed to settle the tie. That was until Tony Cottee scored an extra-time goal for a 1-0 win.

SATURDAY 7TH FEBRUARY 1931

After losing 4-0 at Grimsby earlier in the season, the Hammers were looking for revenge in this home fixture. Flying winger Jimmy Ruffell scored a hat-trick but to the dismay of the home faithful Grimsby Town scored four.

SATURDAY 7TH FEBRUARY 1959

A London derby at Chelsea attracted a huge Stamford Bridge crowd of 52,698 spectators. It was an exciting first half which ended 2-2 with Vic Keeble scoring both the Hammers' goals. In the second half the Blues scored again to finish 3-2 winners.

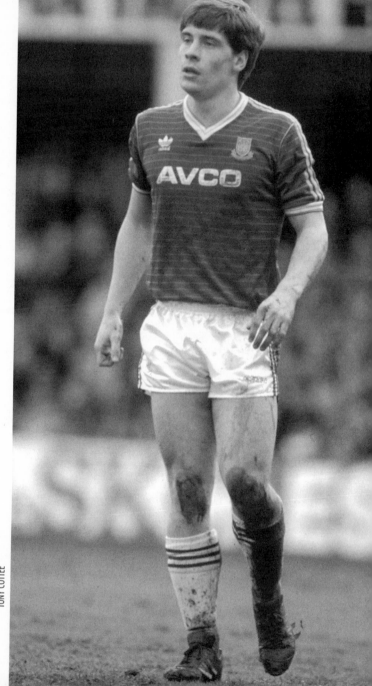

SATURDAY 7TH FEBRUARY 2004

A recent signing from Spurs, Bobby Zamora made his debut for the club. The Hammers were in Yorkshire to play Bradford City in the First Division. One down at half-time, they fought back to equalise through Zamora – who had joined the Hammers in a swap deal involving Jermain Defoe – and late on Marlon Harewood scored West Ham's second for an excellent come-from-behind 2-1 win.

SATURDAY 8TH FEBRUARY 1947

In the first Football League season after the war, the Hammers were at home to Newport County in the Second Division. A smaller than usual attendance of 12,447 watched as West Ham won 3-0. Centre-forward Frank Neary scored twice with the other goal coming from Terry Woodgate.

SATURDAY 8TH FEBRUARY 1964

Every Hammer loves winning a London derby match, and a superb performance against Tottenham Hotspur gave Hammers' fans that winning feeling at Upton Park. On top throughout, the crowd of 36,838 were thrilled by a stylish attacking display from the Hammers. Leading 2-0 at half-time with goals from Geoff Hurst and John Sissons, West Ham added two more in the second half from Ronnie Boyce and Johnny Byrne for a convincing 4-0 victory.

MONDAY 8TH FEBRUARY 1971

Languishing in 20th place in the First Division the Hammers badly needed a win, as they travelled to face Coventry City at Highfield Road. A first-half goal from Jimmy Greaves won the game for West Ham.

SATURDAY 9TH FEBRUARY 1929

After losing 4-1 at Leeds United in September West Ham were looking for revenge in the home First Division fixture. Centre-forward Vic Watson was the hero as he scored an incredible six goals. Also on the scoresheet in the 8-2 rout were Viv Gibbins and Tommy Yews.

TUESDAY 9TH FEBRUARY 1999

Frank Lampard was in the England team for their under-21 game with France at Pride Park. He captained the side to a 2-1 victory.

SATURDAY 10TH FEBRUARY 1900

Half-back Syd Bishop was born in Stepney, London. Between 1920 and 1927 he played in a total of 159 league games for the Hammers, scoring eight goals. Bishop was in the West Ham side that played in the first Wembley FA Cup Final in 1923. He then moved to Leicester City where he gained four caps for England in 1927. He later played for Chelsea between 1928 and 1933, appearing in 103 league games.

SATURDAY 10TH FEBRUARY 1979

Sunderland and West Ham were in the top six of the First Division going into an eagerly awaited clash. It was an exciting afternoon for the 24,998 present at Upton Park who witnessed a 3-3 draw, with David Cross (two) and Pop Robson on target for West Ham.

WEDNESDAY 10TH FEBRUARY 1999

West Ham central defender Rio Ferdinand made his England debut against France at Wembley. He came on as a second half substitute during a 2-0 defeat, under caretaker boss Howard Wilkinson. Ferdinand, who later joined Leeds United and Manchester United for fees totalling nearly £50m, went on to captain his country.

SATURDAY 11TH FEBRUARY 1911

After three successive draws, West Ham finally won by beating Norwich City 2-1. James Rothwell and George Webb were the scorers in this Southern League game played at Upton Park

SATURDAY 11TH FEBRUARY 1933

The Hammers' away form this season was extremely poor and, going into this Second Division game at Bury, they were yet to win on their travels. It was the same old story again as the Shakers won 6-1 in front of a crowd of 7,516. It was Jim Barrett who scored the Hammers' goal.

SATURDAY 11TH FEBRUARY 1967

There was a rare penalty miss by Geoff Hurst in this First Division clash with Sunderland at Upton Park. Johnny Byrne opened the scoring for West Ham and, when Sunderland were leading 2-1 late in the game, it seemed that a home defeat was coming. Then Hurst made up for his penalty miss by heading a goal in the final minute.

SATURDAY 12TH FEBRUARY 2000

A Premiership clash with Bradford City was one of the most exciting games that has been played at Upton Park. After two minutes goalkeeper Shaka Hislop broke his leg and was replaced by young Steve Bywater, who was making his debut. The score was 2-2 at half-time; Trevor Sinclair and John Moncur scored in the first half for the Hammers. Bradford City then scored twice to lead 4-2 – but in a remarkable comeback, West Ham scored three times, through Paolo Di Canio, Frank Lampard and Joe Cole, to win the game 5-4! It was a game that the 25,417 present will never forget.

SATURDAY 12TH FEBRUARY 2011

An amazing comeback by West Ham United at the Hawthorns. West Bromwich Albion were leading 3-0 at half-time but two goals from Demba Ba and one from Carlton Cole made for a thrilling 3-3 draw.

SATURDAY 13TH FEBRUARY 1926

The Hammers were having a poor season and the visit of Bolton Wanderers brought a surprise result. The Trotters were overwhelmingly beaten 6-0 in a display that delighted the crowd of 24,062. Viv Gibbins, Jimmy Ruffell and Vic Watson all scored twice in the rout.

MONDAY 13TH FEBRUARY 1956

On this day in Dublin Irish midfield superstar Liam Brady was born. He made his name with Arsenal, appearing in three consecutive FA Cup Finals and playing in 235 league games, before moving to Italy in 1980. He played for leading sides Juventus, Sampdoria, Inter Milan and finally Ascoli. Brady returned to England in 1987, signing for West Ham, where he made a total of 115 appearances, scoring ten goals. While with West Ham, Brady played 11 times for the Irish Republic to bring his total caps to 72.

SATURDAY 13TH FEBRUARY 1995

Everton were the visitors to Upton Park, and striker Tony Cottee was keen to score against his former club. Cottee was delighted to twice give West Ham the lead, but the Toffees fought back to draw 2-2.

SATURDAY 14TH FEBRUARY 1981

A top-of-the-table clash with rivals Chelsea attracted a crowd of 35,247 to Upton Park for this Second Division game. Thousands were locked out but on the pitch West Ham were on top throughout. The brilliant Brooking scored twice, further goals from Cross and Devonshire giving the Hammers a 4-0 victory.

WEDNESDAY 14TH FEBRUARY 1990

A game which has become known to Hammers as the Valentine's Day massacre. West Ham travelled to Oldham in the League Cup semi-final first-leg. On the difficult plastic pitch at Boundary Park the Hammers were outclassed and overrun, losing 6-0 as 19,263 watched on.

SATURDAY 15TH FEBRUARY 1902

In their second season as a Southern League team, West Ham entertained their London rivals Spurs. A crowd of around 8,000 saw goals from Bill Jenkinson and Rod McEachrane give the Hammers a 2-1 win.

SATURDAY 15TH FEBRUARY 1919

The Hammers travelled to play at The Den – the home of their fiercest rivals Millwall. Even though this was a wartime league game the fixture attracted an attendance of 25,000. It was an equal contest, finishing 2-2 with West Ham goals from Holmes and McCrae.

SATURDAY 15TH FEBRUARY 1975

An exciting home tie in the FA Cup fifth round with Queens Park Rangers saw the visitors go ahead in the first half before Pat Holland equalised. Prompted by Trevor Brooking, the Hammers came out on top when Keith Robson scored the winner.

FRIDAY 16TH FEBRUARY 1934

One of the most popular players to have worn the claret & blue was Ken Brown who was born on this day in Forest Gate, east London. Ken was a West Ham player from 1952 until 1967, playing in 386 league games and 69 Cup ties. He gained one England cap – against Northern Ireland in 1959 – and winners' medals in the 1964 FA Cup Final and in the European Cup Winners' Cup Final in 1965. He later played for Torquay United and was manager at both Norwich City and Plymouth Argyle.

SATURDAY 16TH FEBRUARY 1946

Professional football had returned after the Second World War and there were 15,000 inside Upton Park for this league game with Plymouth Argyle. It was a good day for centre-forward Don Travis who was making his debut as he scored four goals. Also with a hat-trick in this 7-0 win was winger Terry Woodgate.

SATURDAY 16TH FEBRUARY 1991

Third Division Crewe Alexandra came to Upton Park for this Fifth Round FA Cup tie. They made it tough for the Hammers who just scraped through with a late goal from substitute Jimmy Quinn.

SATURDAY 17TH FEBRUARY 1912

A Southern League match with Exeter City brought 10,000 spectators to Upton Park. Danny Shea had scored twice at Exeter earlier in the season and he did it again in this match. The other goal came from Fred Harrison in a 3-2 victory.

TUESDAY 17TH FEBRUARY 2004

Nigel Reo-Coker played for the England under-21 team in their 3-2 friendly game with Holland at Hull City's KC Stadium.

MONDAY 18TH FEBRUARY 1985

Future West Ham player and England under-21 international Anton Ferdinand – younger brother of Rio – was born in Peckham, London. He eventually followed in his brother's footsteps by playing in the West Ham youth team and graduating to the first team and playing for the Hammers in the Premiership.

SATURDAY 18TH FEBRUARY 1990

In goal for West Ham at Swindon Town was Ludek Miklosko, who was making his debut. There were 14,993 at the County Ground to see Jimmy Quinn score twice in the 2-2 draw.

WEDNESDAY 18TH FEBRUARY 2004

Gaining his 61st cap for Wales was Andy Melville, playing against Scotland at Cardiff in their 4-0 win. Included in the Scotland team was Christian Dailly.

SATURDAY 19TH FEBRUARY 1927

Having won 3-1 at West Bromwich Albion in October, West Ham were expected to win this home game with the Baggies. The Albion were bottom of the league but caused an upset by winning 2-1. The 18,231 home faithful had only a goal from Vic Watson to cheer.

SATURDAY 19TH FEBRUARY 1966

An easy win for West Ham in their First Division home encounter with Sheffield United. It was one-way traffic after the Blades gave West Ham the lead with an own-goal from Reg Matthewson after just eight minutes. The 21,238 fans were treated to further goals from Peter Brabrook, Martin Peters and Geoff Hurst in this 4-0 victory.

SATURDAY 20TH FEBRUARY 1958

Promotion-chasing West Ham were away to their near neighbours Leyton Orient for this Second Division fixture. The Hammers were too strong for their London rivals and ran out easy 4-1 winners. Top scorers in that promotion-winning season Johnny Dick and Vic Keeble both scored; the other goals came from Billy Dare and John Smith.

SATURDAY 20TH FEBRUARY 1982

After four successive away defeats the Hammers travelled to play the league leaders Southampton. They went behind early on but levelled with a penalty from Ray Stewart. The Saints were inspired by Kevin Keegan and it was Mick Channon who scored their winner.

SATURDAY 20TH FEBRUARY 1999

Hammers' fans will confirm, a trip to Anfield to play Liverpool usually means a defeat. However, on this occasion a creditable 2-2 draw was gained. The Hammers were twice behind but Frank Lampard scored from a penalty and Marc Keller scored the other direct from a corner!

SATURDAY 21ST FEBRUARY 1987

Cup fever! The fifth round of the FA Cup had seen West Ham drawn away to Sheffield Wednesday. Frank McAvennie scored to give the Hammers the lead at Hillsborough, but the Owls preserved a 14-year unbeaten home record in the competition as they equalised for a 1-1 draw – and the cup dream ended when West Ham lost the replay 2-0.

FRANK McAVENNIE

SATURDAY 21st FEBRUARY 1998

Trevor Sinclair scored to give the Hammers the lead at Bolton Wanderers in this Premiership fixture and West Ham looked to be cruising to an away win – but John Hartson was sent off and the Wanderers equalised with just four minutes remaining.

SATURDAY 22nd FEBRUARY 1902

A Southern League home game with Queens Park Rangers before 4,000 spectators saw both Fergus Hunt and George Radcliffe score twice to give West Ham a convincing 4-0 win.

SATURDAY 22nd FEBRUARY 1975

West Ham had lost at Molineux without scoring for the previous six years. So it was no surprise when the Wolves raced into a 3-0 lead. However, Bobby Gould scored a late consolation goal for the Hammers.

TUESDAY 22nd FEBRUARY 2000

Joe Cole made his England under-21 debut against Argentina at Craven Cottage. He came on as a second half substitute in the 1-0 win. Captaining the team was Cole's Hammers team-mate Frank Lampard, who set up the winning goal.

FRIDAY 23rd FEBRUARY 2001

Sven-Göran Eriksson picks his first England squad for the friendly against Spain at Villa Park. Included in the squad are Hammers Michael Carrick, Frank Lampard and Joe Cole.

SATURDAY 24th FEBRUARY 1940

John Lyall was born in Ilford in Essex and went on to become the club's greatest ever manager. He started his career at West Ham, playing in the youth team in 1957. After making his first team debut in 1960 he went on to play a total of 34 games before injury ended his playing career. He then worked in the office before becoming the first team coach. In 1974 he was named as the team manager and went on to lead West Ham when they won the FA Cup in 1975 and 1980. When West Ham were relegated in 1989 the club dispensed with his services and he became the manager at Ipswich Town for a few seasons. It was a very sad day in April 2006 when John died as his family and friends had lost a wonderful man.

SUNDAY 24TH FEBRUARY 1991

Entertaining rivals Millwall, the crowd of 20,503 were looking for a fierce encounter. Tony Gale broke his nose in a collision with Teddy Sheringham. The Hammers responded, winning the game 3-1 with two goals from Frank McAvennie and one from Trevor Morley.

MONDAY 24TH FEBRUARY 1997

West Ham were struggling and badly needed to win this home fixture with Tottenham Hotspur. It was an amazing game played in howling wind and rain throughout. The goals flowed from both teams; it was 3-2 at half-time with new signings Kitson and Hartson scoring and one from Dicks. In the second half Spurs equalised only for Julian Dicks to get the winner from the penalty spot.

SATURDAY 25TH FEBRUARY 1956

The Hammers hadn't won since December and faced a home game with Liverpool in the Second Division. A crowd of 18,798 were pleased to see a 2-0 win. Both goals were own-goals courtesy of Liverpool defenders Geoff Twentyman and John Molyneux.

SATURDAY 25TH FEBRUARY 1978

West Ham found themselves 2-0 down at half-time in a home First Division game with London rivals Arsenal. But a spirited fight-back saw second-half goals from Alan Taylor and David Cross rescue a draw.

WEDNESDAY 25TH FEBRUARY 1998

West Ham travelled to Blackburn Rovers for an FA Cup fifth round replay. A dour struggle went into extra-time. John Hartson scored for the Hammers but Blackburn equalised for the tie to go to penalties. The hero was goalkeeper Craig Forrest who saved the last spot-kick which gave West Ham a 5-4 shootout win.

SATURDAY 26TH FEBRUARY 1994

A home clash with Manchester United in a charged atmosphere. United scored early but the Hammers bounced back with two goals in two second half minutes, from Chapman and Morley. Just as West Ham thought they would win the match Ince popped up to equalise three minutes from the end.

SATURDAY 26TH FEBRUARY 2000

A disaster at home to Everton. On-loan keeper Sasa Ilic gifted the Merseysiders two of their four goals. Toffee Nick Barmby scored a hat-trick in the 4-0 win and sent most of the 26,025 crowd home unhappy.

SATURDAY 27TH FEBRUARY 1965

Liverpool came to Upton Park with an unbeaten run of 21 games and at half-time they were leading 1-0. Then full-back Eddie Presland scored on his debut and, five minutes later, Geoff Hurst scored the winner.

SATURDAY 27TH FEBRUARY 1971

A First Division league game with the Hammers away to Blackpool, with both clubs fighting relegation. Blackpool scored after 26 seconds, but Geoff Hurst equalised with a penalty late on for a 1-1 draw.

SUNDAY 27TH FEBRUARY 2000

Craig Forrest saved a penalty playing for Canada in the CONCACAF Gold Cup Final, as Canada beat Colombia 2-0 in Los Angeles.

SATURDAY 28TH FEBRUARY 1925

West Ham's forwards were on form when they travelled to Lancashire to face Burnley at Turf Moor, scoring four goals. Unfortunately the Hammers' defence was poor as they conceded five in the 5-4 defeat!

SATURDAY 28TH FEBRUARY 1981

The Hammers were Second Division leaders going into this game at Watford. Leading scorer David Cross scored twice, taking his tally to 27 for the season, in a 2-1 win.

SATURDAY 29TH FEBRUARY 1964

A lockout at Upton Park, with 36,651 crammed in for a sixth round FA Cup tie with Burnley. West Ham won 3-2, as Johnny Byrne scored twice, with another goal coming from 17-year-old winger John Sissons.

TUESDAY 29TH FEBRUARY 1972

Sheffield United hadn't won for seven games and earlier in the season had been hammered 5-0 by West Ham in the League Cup. But they took revenge. Billy Dearden scored a hat-trick in a 3-0 win at Bramall Lane.

WEST HAM UNITED
On This Day

MARCH

SATURDAY 1st MARCH 1947

Struggling Swansea Town came to London for this Second Division game. New signing Frank Neary scored twice for the Hammers and Almer Hall added another in a 3-0 win.

SATURDAY 1st MARCH 1980

With both teams going for promotion to the top division there was a big crowd of 20,040 at Kenilworth Road for the match with Luton Town. The home side scored after only three minutes and it took a penalty scored by Ray Stewart late in the game to level the scores at 1-1.

SATURDAY 1st MARCH 2003

The Hammers were 19th in the Premiership going into a home game with Tottenham Hotspur. Roared on by a crowd of 35,049, ex-Spurs striker Les Ferdinand netted in the first half. Michael Carrick scored a rare goal in the second half to give the Hammers a much-needed 2-0 win.

SATURDAY 2nd MARCH 1935

A visit to Swansea where the teams shared nine goals. Unfortunately for West Ham, Swansea got five of them. The Hammers' goalscorers were Joe Foxall (two), John Morton and Tommy Tippett.

SATURDAY 2nd MARCH 1963

The Hammers had not won at home since October and this did not change with the visit of Arsenal. The Gunners were 2-0 up at half-time and ran out convincing 4-0 winners in a First Division fixture.

SATURDAY 2nd MARCH 1974

The home clash with Chelsea brought 34,143 fans to the ground. A game that needed a hero and the Hammers' skipper was that man. The courageous Billy Bonds rallied his troops and went on to score a hat-trick. The Blues were well beaten in this 3-0 success.

SATURDAY 3rd MARCH 1956

The sixth round of the FA Cup paired West Ham with their rivals Tottenham Hotspur. The tie at White Hart Lane attracted a crowd of 69,111 who witnessed a thriller. Johnny Dick bagged a hat-trick in a thrilling 3-3 draw. The replay saw the Hammers beaten 2-1.

WEDNESDAY 3RD MARCH 1976

For the first-leg of this European Cup Winners' Cup match the Hammers had to travel to Holland where they met Den Haag. In a torrid first half West Ham were left trailing 4-0 at half-time with two of the goals coming from disputed penalties. They fought back after the interval and Billy Jennings scored twice to give West Ham a chance in the second-leg.

SATURDAY 4TH MARCH 1972

Struggling Huddersfield Town were the visitors in this First Division game, in which West Ham gained revenge for a recent FA Cup defeat by the Yorkshiremen. Centre-forward Clyde Best added two goals and one from Pop Robson saw the Hammers win 3-0.

WEDNESDAY 4TH MARCH 1981

Russians Dynamo Tbilisi were at Upton Park for a first-leg quarter-final tie in the European Cup Winners' Cup tie. A brilliant display of football saw them win 4-1. The Hammers' consolation goal came from David Cross. A sporting crowd of 34,957 applauded the Russians off the pitch. Tbilisi went on to win the trophy.

SATURDAY 5TH MARCH 1960

Everton arrived at Upton Park without an away win and were soon trailing to an early goal from John Bond – but the visitors scored twice in the second half and it took a late goal from John Dick just before the end that salvaged a 2-2 draw.

SATURDAY 5TH MARCH 1966

Having won at Aston Villa earlier that season, the Hammers were looking for a First Division double over them in this home game. A rare goal from Jack Burkett and three others from Peter Brabrook, Johnny Byrne and Geoff Hurst gave West Ham a 4-2 victory.

SATURDAY 6TH MARCH 1937

Not much joy for the 8,079 fans at Doncaster Rovers when they entertained West Ham. The Rovers were bottom of the league and suffered a 4-1 defeat. Scoring for the Hammers were Joe Foxall, Len Goulden, Sam Small and John Morton.

SATURDAY 6TH MARCH 1943

A wartime cup game against Watford. West Ham fielded George Gladwin – a guest player from Manchester United – and there was a crowd of approximately 2,000 at Upton Park to see a 6-1 home win. A brace of goals were scored by Richard Dunn, George Foreman and Len Goulden.

SATURDAY 6TH MARCH 1993

An emotional day at Upton Park with 25,000 inside the ground for the visit of Wolverhampton Wanderers to pay their respects to Bobby Moore who had sadly died a week earlier. Before the kick-off, Geoff Hurst and Martin Peters – accompanied by Ron Greenwood – carried to the centre spot a giant number six shirt made of claret and blue flowers. The teams came out, heads bowed, and observed a minute's silence. The game itself was not a spectacle but it was fitting that West Ham won 3-1.

MONDAY 7TH MARCH 1927

A rare Monday afternoon game with Arsenal – which perhaps explains the paltry attendance of just 11,764. Those supporters present witnessed an excellent performance from the Hammers, as Arsenal were outclassed and beaten 7-0. Centre-forward Vic Watson scored a hat-trick and other goals were scored by Joe Johnson and Jimmy Ruffell while there were two own-goals.

SATURDAY 7TH MARCH 1936

A top-of-the-table clash with Manchester United at Upton Park drew a capacity gate. Not unusual to have a bumper attendance for this fixture, but this was a Second Division match. Having won earlier that season in Manchester, the Hammers were looking for a double. But despite a goal from Len Goulden they lost 2-1.

SATURDAY 7TH MARCH 1981

Going into the home game with Newcastle United, the Hammers were unbeaten in eight league games in the Second Division and looking a very good bet for promotion back to the First Division. A goal from David Cross was enough to give West Ham a 1-0 win which gave them a ten-point lead at the top of the table.

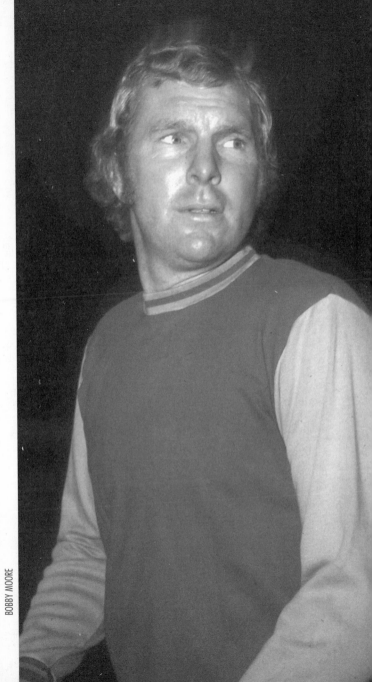

BOBBY MOORE

SATURDAY 8TH MARCH 1958

League leaders West Ham welcomed Rotherham to Upton Park for a Second Division match. The Yorkshiremen were crushed in a brilliant display of attacking football. Top scorer Johnny Dick scored four with Vic Keeble and John Smith both scoring twice. The 8-0 scoreline was the Hammers' biggest-ever league victory.

SATURDAY 8TH MARCH 1975

A sixth-round FA Cup tie away to Arsenal drew an attendance of 56,742 to Highbury – but it was the Hammers supporters who went home happy! Hero was striker Alan Taylor who had been signed from Rochdale earlier that season. Taylor scored both goals in a 2-0 victory, with West Ham on their way to Wembley.

SATURDAY 9TH MARCH 1912

A visit to The Den to play rivals Millwall in the Southern League and, before the Lions' biggest crowd of the season, the Hammers were well beaten 5-1. The West Ham goal came in the second half from centre-forward Fred Harrison.

WEDNESDAY 9TH MARCH 1966

In 1966 the League Cup Final was played over two legs at the home of the two finalists – the first Wembley final was a year later in 1967. On this occasion the Hammers hosted West Bromwich Albion in the first-leg. Albion took the lead but Bobby Moore equalised and Johnny Byrne won the game when he scored in the last minute.

TUESDAY 9TH MARCH 1993

Grimsby Town were the visitors for this Second Division game. The Hammers had been unbeaten in 14 league games and extended their run to 15 with a 2-1 win. Captain Julian Dicks scored both the goals – but also conceded a penalty which Grimsby missed.

SATURDAY 10TH MARCH 1945

The Hammers' third meeting of the 1944/45 season with Queens Park Rangers. A home game in the Football League South Cup Group ended 5-0 in the Hammers' favour, with 20,000 there to see goals from Charlie Whitchurch (two), Len Goulden (two) and Sam Small.

SATURDAY 10TH MARCH 1956

Both Hammers' wingers were goalscorers on this day. Harry Hooper and Ken Tucker got the goals in the 2-1 home league victory against Bristol Rovers.

SATURDAY 10TH MARCH 1990

A home Second Division game with Portsmouth turned out to be a hard-fought 2-1 win for West Ham. Losing 1-0, they came back with goals from Trevor Morley and Julian Dicks who scored from the penalty spot.

SATURDAY 11TH MARCH 1905

The 1904/05 season was the first West Ham played at Upton Park – but the fixture with Watford attracted a smaller-than-usual crowd of around 3,000 fans. The Hammers won this Southern League game 2-0, as Billy Bridgeman and Chris Carrick both scored.

SATURDAY 11TH MARCH 1939

Having lost 6-0 at Millwall the previous Saturday, Norwich City were hoping for better things when they entertained West Ham, but there was more disappointment for the majority of the 15,027 fans as the Hammers won 6-2. Sammy Small scored a hat-trick, Joe Foxall netted twice and the other goal came from Jackie Morton.

SATURDAY 11TH MARCH 1961

Preston North End were languishing at the foot of the First Division but the Hammers were in for a shock on this visit to Deepdale. The 12,084 home fans saw their favourites beat West Ham 4-0 – but it didn't help them avoid the drop as they went down with Newcastle.

SATURDAY 12TH MARCH 1966

West Ham were enjoying a fine home run, but the First Division's bottom club Blackburn Rovers were winning 1-0 at half-time during their visit to Upton Park. But in the space of three second-half minutes the Hammers scored three goals from Brian Dear, Peter Brabrook and Geoff Hurst. Full-back Jack Burkett added another for an impressive 4-1 win – and his goal meant it was the fourth successive home game in which the Hammers had scored four goals.

WEDNESDAY 12TH MARCH 1997

West Ham were fighting relegation from the Premiership – but a London derby with Chelsea at Upton Park proved a thriller. Down 1-0 at half-time, the Hammers equalised with a penalty by Julian Dicks. Paul Kitson then put West Ham ahead, only for Chelsea to equalise with three minutes remaining. However, Upton Park erupted as Kitson scored the winner in the final minute of the match!

SATURDAY 13TH MARCH 1937

A Second Division home game with neighbours Fulham, and it was an exciting 3-3 draw for the 29,405 spectators. The West Ham goals came from John Morton, Len Goulden and Sammy Small.

SATURDAY 13TH MARCH 1943

West Ham travelled south to play Brighton and Hove Albion in a wartime Football League South Cup game. The crowd of 7,521 saw the Hammers triumph 4-1. Centre-forward George Foreman grabbed a hat trick with Jackie Wood scoring the other goal.

SATURDAY 13TH MARCH 1999

The Hammers were away to Chelsea who had not been beaten at home in the Premiership all season – but Harry Redknapp's men changed all that. Paul Kitson scored the only goal of the game to win all three points at Stamford Bridge.

SATURDAY 14TH MARCH 1964

Superbly marshalled by Bobby Moore, the Hammers put on a wonderful performance in beating Manchester United in the FA Cup semi-final. In driving rain at Hillsborough, midfielder Ronnie Boyce scored twice; Geoff Hurst got the other in the 3-1 win.

FRIDAY 14TH MARCH 1969

A 29,053 crowd was at Upton Park for this Friday fixture with Coventry City, managed by Hammers legend Noel Cantwell. Johnny Sissons scored after two minutes and set the tone for a sparkling West Ham performance which saw them run out 5-2 winners. There were two penalties both converted by Geoff Hurst. The other scorers were Billy Bonds and Hurst's England colleague Martin Peters.

SATURDAY 14TH MARCH 1981

There were 100,000 at Wembley for the League Cup Final against Liverpool. After 90 minutes the score was 0-0 and the tie went into extra-time – but there was controversy when Liverpool scored through Alan Kennedy when Sammy Lee was in an off-side position. With a minute to go Alvin Martin's header was handled and from the resultant penalty Ray Stewart scored to force a replay.

SATURDAY 15TH MARCH 1919

As the final wartime season of World War I came to an end the biggest crowd of the season – totalling 26,000 – flocked to Upton Park for the visit of Chelsea. It was an exciting game which ended all square at 3-3. Guest player Sam Chedgzoy, from Everton, scored twice with Syd Puddefoot claiming the other.

SATURDAY 15TH MARCH 1947

It's a good day for centre-forward Frank Neary when he faced West Bromwich Albion at Upton Park. The Hammers won 3-2 and in doing so scored three goals for the third successive home game. In each of the previous two games Neary had scored twice but this time he went one better by scoring a hat-trick. He finished the season with 15 goals in his 14 appearances.

SATURDAY 16TH MARCH 1940

In the first season of wartime football the Hammers faced the trip across London to play Arsenal. There were 10,371 spectators at Highbury to see West Ham pull off a fine 3-2 victory. Ted Fenton, who later became the West Ham manager, scored twice with George Foreman adding the other goal.

TUESDAY 16TH MARCH 1965

West Ham travelled to Switzerland to play Lausanne in the European Cup Winners' Cup quarter-final first-leg. Centre-forward Brian Dear scored in the first half and Johnny Byrne went on a brilliant 50-yard run to score an excellent second – and although the Swiss pulled a goal back late in the game – it was a good night's work for Ron Greenwood's men, as the match finished 2-1 in favour of the Hammers.

SATURDAY 16th MARCH 2002

An amazing game: an eight-goal thriller with league leaders Manchester United at Upton Park, who went home with all three points. Twice West Ham took the lead through Steve Lomas and Fredi Kanoute, but the Red Devils equalised and then went two goals ahead. Jermain Defoe pulled a goal back to make it 4-3 – but David Beckham scored a fifth for Manchester United, a penalty, with a minute to go.

SUNDAY 17th MARCH 1935

Goalkeeper Lawrie Leslie was born in Edinburgh. In 1958 he joined Hibernian and was in the Hibs side that lost to Clyde in the Scottish FA Cup Final. He was then transferred to Airdrie where he won five international caps for Scotland. Lawrie joined West Ham in 1961 and proved himself to be a fearless goalkeeper. He played in 61 games for the club before joining Stoke City in 1963, where he played for three seasons. He finally ended his playing career at Southend United and he later became a coach at Millwall.

SATURDAY 17th MARCH 1973

Centre-forward Ted MacDougall – a big money signing from Manchester United – netted his first goal for the club on his home debut. The Hammers were playing Manchester City and won the the First Division fixture 2-1. It was leading scorer Pop Robson who added the second goal.

SATURDAY 18th MARCH 1933

West Ham were struggling in the Second Division when they met Everton in the FA Cup Semi-Final at Molineux. They gave a good account of themselves but lost 2-1 to the eventual cup winners. Top scorer Vic Watson netted the Hammers' goal.

SATURDAY 18th MARCH 1950

Bury and West Ham were hovering just above the Second Division relegation zone when they met at Upton Park. The encounter only attracted 15,835 fans who had endured a long, hard season. On this occasion they were sent home happy, however, as Gerry Gazzard, Derek Parker, Eric Parsons and Terry Woodgate got the goals in a 4-0 win. It was West Ham's last victory of the season – but both sides survived.

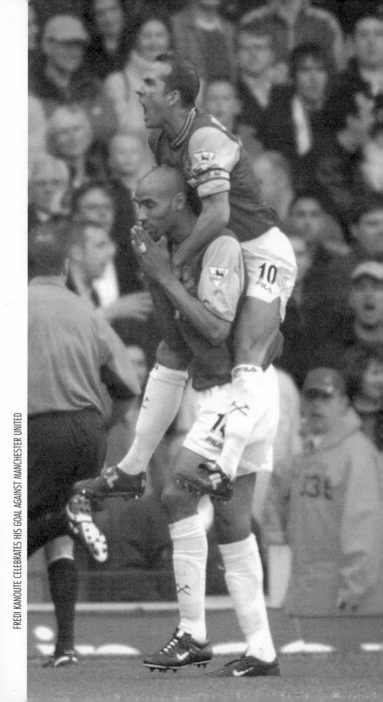

SATURDAY 18TH MARCH 1973

A home First Division game against Nottingham Forest saw the Hammers lead 3-0 after 30 minutes. Pop Robson netted two, with the other from Geoff Hurst. Forest came back with two goals, but Trevor Brooking killed off any potential comeback when he added a fourth, a minute from time, to seal a 4-2 victory.

SATURDAY 19TH MARCH 1927

Struggling Manchester United attracted a crowd of 18,347 to Old Trafford for their game with West Ham. The Hammers had beaten United 4-0 in London earlier in the season. They were therefore pleased to do the double, winning 3-0. In sparkling form was Vic Watson – who scored twice – with the other coming from Bill Johnson.

SATURDAY 19TH MARCH 1988

It was only a second win in 11 matches for West Ham as they beat Watford 1-0 at Upton Park in the First Division. Making his debut was centre-forward Leroy Rosenior who had just been signed from Fulham. He was an instant hit as he scored the winning goal in the second half.

MONDAY 20TH MARCH 1961

Nottingham was the birthplace of striker Trevor Morley, a big striker who started his playing career at Northampton Town in 1985 where he played for three seasons, making a total of 107 appearances scoring 39 goals. He then joined Manchester City in 1988 where he played in 32 league games and scored 14 goals. Trevor came to West Ham in 1989 and became a big favourite with the fans. He spent six seasons at Upton Park making a total of 215 appearances and scoring 70 goals. He later had a few seasons at Reading before moving into management in Norway.

SATURDAY 20TH MARCH 1971

The home game with Ipswich Town provided good entertainment for the 25,957 spectators at Upton Park. The game ended 2-2 with the Hammers' goals coming from two typical smash-and-grab efforts from Jimmy Greaves. Both Frank Lampard and Ronnie Boyce hit the Ipswich woodwork.

SATURDAY 21st MARCH 1959

The crowd of 27,722 witnessed an exciting game with Bolton Wanderers at Upton Park, with both teams in the top six of the First Division at the time. It was a sixth successive home victory for the Hammers as they won 4-3. In a very successful experiment, full-back John Bond had been moved to centre-forward, from where he scored twice. The other two goals came from Johnny Dick and Harry Obeney.

SATURDAY 21st MARCH 1970

There was a genuine buzz of excitement amongst the West Ham supporters who travelled to Manchester City on this day, as legendary goalscorer Jimmy Greaves was to make his debut. Greaves had a habit of always scoring on his debut, and in typical fashion he scored twice in a 5-1 win. Geoff Hurst also scored twice and Ronnie Boyce scored with a stunning volley from the half-way line.

WEDNESDAY 21st MARCH 1990

The Hammers were at home to an in-form Sheffield United who had not lost since January, but an excellent display from West Ham saw Stuart Slater in sparkling form, setting up two goals. Jimmy Quinn grabbed a hat-trick and it was a rout as the Hammers scored two more – from Trevor Morley and Martin Allen – to win 5-0.

SATURDAY 22nd MARCH 1930

Leeds United travelled to Upton Park in fear of centre-forward Vic Watson. Earlier in the season he had scored two against them in the league and four goals against them in the FA Cup. There was an attendance of 18,351 to see West Ham win 3-0, this time in the First Division. Again, it was Watson who scored all three goals.

FRIDAY 22nd MARCH 1940

West Ham were visitors at The Dell for a Football League South game with Southampton. Although this was the first wartime season, the Hammers had been able to field settled sides. On this occasion they proved too good for the Saints in winning 6-1. George Foreman and Sam Small both scored twice and one goal each came from Benny Fenton and Len Goulden.

SATURDAY 23RD MARCH 1963

This game at Bolton was played, unusually, on a Saturday evening. The Hammers lost 3-0 and they might have had their mind on the following weekend when they were to meet Liverpool in the FA Cup.

SATURDAY 23RD MARCH 1996

The home game with Manchester City proved good value for the crowd of 24,017. It was all-action as Ludek Miklosko saved a penalty and Steve Lomas was sent off. Iain Dowie scored two headers and further goals came from Julian Dicks and Dani in a 4-2 win.

SATURDAY 24TH MARCH 1923

West Ham played Derby County at Stamford Bridge in the FA Cup semi-final. The Hammers were in the Second Division at the time but put on a good display for the 50,795 spectators, to win 5-2 and reach the first Wembley Cup Final. Billy Brown and Billy Moore both scored two; winger Jimmy Ruffell added the other.

FRIDAY 24TH MARCH 1978

Having gone seven games without a win, the Hammers badly needed to beat Ipswich Town at Upton Park in this Good Friday First Division fixture. It was stalemate at half-time but the second half belonged to David Cross who scored a fine hat-trick with two headers and an angled shot to give the home side a 3-0 victory.

SATURDAY 24TH MARCH 1979

A Second Division home game with Newcastle United brought an attendance of 24,650. The Hammers hadn't scored in their previous three games, but more than made up for it as Trevor Brooking was the architect in a 5-0 win. John McDowell scored twice, with Alan Devonshire, Frank Lampard and Pop Robson also on the scoresheet.

SATURDAY 25TH MARCH 1978

West Ham and Chelsea were both struggling near the bottom of the First Division prior to this derby at Upton Park. The Blues were leading 1-0 until the last ten minutes when, to the delight of the home faithful, the Hammers scored three. Trevor Brooking, Bill Green, with his only goal for the club, and Pat Holland were the scorers.

SATURDAY 25TH MARCH 1989

The Hammers were bottom of the league and had just been knocked out of the FA Cup by Norwich City when they travelled to play mid-table Aston Villa – but they got the boost they wanted when Paul Ince scored a wonder goal. He ran 60 yards with the ball and scored from 30 yards. It was enough to secure three points but at the end of the season West Ham were relegated.

SATURDAY 26TH MARCH 1927

Both West Ham and Bolton Wanderers were in the First Division's top six when they met at Upton Park. There were only 17,752 present but those who came were rewarded with plenty of goals. The game ended in a 4-4 draw with the Hammers' scorers being Stan Earle, Vic Watson and Jimmy Ruffell (two).

SATURDAY 26TH MARCH 2000

In the home game with Wimbledon, Paolo Di Canio scored one of the best goals ever seen at the Boleyn Ground. Nine minutes had passed when a cross came over from Trevor Sinclair and the Italian hit a volley in mid-air – it was a goal of pure genius. Fredi Kanoute made it 2-0 before the visitors pulled a goal back with the game ending 2-1 in the Hammers' favour.

FRIDAY 27TH MARCH 1964

A Good Friday home game with Stoke City saw the return of goalkeeper Lawrie Leslie – now with the Potteries club – and he was soon picking the ball out of the net as Bobby Moore scored after two minutes. The Hammers then went on to win 4-1 with further goals from Peter Brabrook, Ronnie Boyce and Johnny Byrne.

WEDNESDAY 27TH MARCH 1996

In the Northern Ireland team which lost 2-0 to Norway in Belfast were three Hammers: Keith Rowland, Michael Hughes and Iain Dowie, who was sent off during the defeat.

WEDNESDAY 27TH MARCH 2002

England lost 2-1 to Italy in a friendly at Elland Road. Trevor Sinclair played from the start while David James and Joe Cole came on as subs.

SATURDAY 28TH MARCH 1903

Luton Town were the opponents for this Southern League match, and the 4-1 win turned out to be the Hammers' biggest of the season. Curiously, the attendance of 800 was the smallest. Leading goalscorer Billy Grassam scored twice with one each for James Bigden and John Farrell.

SATURDAY 29TH MARCH 1958

League leaders West Ham were chasing promotion and travelled to Stoke City in determined mood. They came away with all the points having won 4-1; leading scorer Johnny Dick scored two with the other two from Vic Keeble and Mike Grice.

SATURDAY 29TH MARCH 1986

The Hammers were enjoying their best season for many years as they challenged for the First Division title. They took the short trip to Stamford Bridge and humbled Chelsea 4-0. It was a vintage performance with goals from Alan Devonshire, two from Tony Cottee, and a volley from Frank McAvennie completing the rout.

SATURDAY 30TH MARCH 1940

There were around 10,000 inside Stamford Bridge as Chelsea entertained West Ham in a wartime league fixture. It turned out to be an amazing game as the Hammers won 10-3; Sammy Small scored four, Ted Fenton three, George Foreman two and the final goalscorer Joe Foxall.

SATURDAY 30TH MARCH 1974

West Ham were in relegation trouble and knew a home game with league leaders Leeds United would be tough. After Leeds took the lead the Hammers fought back to shatter the Yorkshiremen with three goals. Clyde Best, Trevor Brooking and Pop Robson were the delighted scorers as West Ham clinched a vital win which helped them eventually secure First Division status.

SATURDAY 31ST MARCH 1970

A home First Division game with Wolves saw Jimmy Greaves score after two minutes with a header. The Hammers were on top throughout and added further goals from Billy Bonds and Bobby Howe to win 3-0.

WEST HAM UNITED
On This Day

APRIL

SATURDAY 1st APRIL 1972

West Ham became the first Football League club to field three black players in the same match in the home game against Tottenham Hotspur. The trio were Clyde Best, Ade Coker and Clive Charles. The match was also significant as Trevor Brooking scored Goal of the Season with a 20-yard lob. Coker added another to complete the 2-0 victory.

WEDNESDAY 1st APRIL 1981

The League Cup Final replay against Liverpool at Villa Park. A crowd of 36,693 saw Paul Goddard put West Ham in front after ten minutes. Kenny Dalglish equalised on 26 minutes. Three minutes later Alan Hansen added a second for the Reds, which turned out to be the winner.

SATURDAY 1st APRIL 2000

League leaders Manchester United entertain West Ham before 61,611 fans at Old Trafford. Paulo Wanchope gave the Hammers a shock lead after 11 minutes, but this provoked a fierce reaction from United who came back with seven goals which included a Paul Scholes hat-trick.

TUESDAY 1st APRIL 2003

Joe Cole and Jermain Defoe were both in the England under-21 team that drew 1-1 against Turkey at St James' Park, Newcastle.

MONDAY 2nd APRIL 1923

Already FA Cup finalists, West Ham continued a fine season. A trip to Bury saw them stay on course for promotion to the First Division with a 5-2 win. Legendary centre-forward Vic Watson scored twice with further goals coming from Billy Moore, Dick Richards and Jimmy Ruffell.

WEDNESDAY 2nd APRIL 2003

In goal for England against Turkey at Sunderland was David James. The European Championship game was won 2-0 by the hosts.

SATURDAY 3rd APRIL 1943

A wartime cup game saw Brighton & Hove Albion visit Upton Park. The south coast visitors were well beaten 7-1 with 5,500 spectators watching on. England international Len Goulden scored a hat-trick, with other goals coming from Woodgate, Foreman, Walker and an own-goal.

SATURDAY 3rd APRIL 1971

With the Hammers hoping to avoid relegation, there was an attendance of 38,507 for the home game against Manchester United. Roared on by the home faithful, the Hammers raced into a two-goal lead courtesy of Geoff Hurst and Pop Robson. Although George Best scored in the second half, West Ham held on to win 2-1.

SATURDAY 3rd APRIL 1993

A trip to the Midlands to play lowly Birmingham City in a Second Division fixture. It was the Blues who went ahead and, with three minutes to go, were still leading 1-0. Then, in an amazing finish, a piledriver from Kenny Brown and a dipping shot from Ian Bishop gave the Hammers a 2-1 win.

WEDNESDAY 4th APRIL 1973

Centre-half Paul Heffer – after 17 games for the club – had to retire from playing due to an injury. He was granted a testimonial game against the Israeli national team. The game at Upton Park attracted a crowd of 7,465 and saw the Hammers win an entertaining match 3-2.

MONDAY 4th APRIL 1994

The Hammers' fans in the 31,502 crowd at White Hart Lane were ecstatic. Tottenham were losing 1-0 at half-time after Steve Jones had scored. There was further misery for Spurs in the second half when the Hammers scored three more times with goals from Morley (two) and Marsh. Tottenham's consolation goal came from Sheringham.

SATURDAY 5th APRIL 1913

Old rivals Millwall and West Ham met at The Den before the Lions' biggest gate of the season. The Hammers were unbeaten since January and that form continued as they won 3-1. Skipper Tom Randall scored his first goal of the season with Ashton and Bailey the other marksmen.

WEDNESDAY 5th APRIL 1966

A big night at Upton Park as Borussia Dortmund visit in the European Cup Winners' Cup semi-final first-leg. Martin Peters opens the scoring in the second half but the Germans score twice in the final five minutes to go away with a 2-1 advantage.

TUESDAY 5TH APRIL 1983

West Ham travelled to Wales for the return First Division fixture with Swansea City. Swans scored after just two minutes. However, inspired by Alan Devonshire, the Hammers hit back with five goals. Geoff Pike and Alan Dickens bagged a brace apiece with Devonshire scoring one in a 5-1 win – the second win during the Easter period.

SATURDAY 6TH APRIL 1918

The final home game in the wartime London Combination League against Crystal Palace. Centre-forward Syd Puddefoot was outstanding in this extraordinary 11-0 rout. A home crowd of 4,000 were amazed as Puddefoot scored seven goals with further strikes added by Andrew Cunningham, Herbert Ashton and two from a guest player listed only as Burke. The Hammers scored a total of 103 league goals that season and finished runners-up to Chelsea.

SATURDAY 6TH APRIL 1940

During the Second World War George Foreman scored an amazing 188 goals for the Hammers in the various league and cup competitions. On this occasion West Ham were playing Tottenham at White Hart Lane and won 6-2. Full-back Charlie Bicknell scored a rare goal with another coming from Len Goulden. However star of the show was Foreman who netted four of those goals that day.

SATURDAY 6TH APRIL 1968

Nineteen-year-old Trevor Brooking came into the side in place of the injured Geoff Hurst. The Hammers were at home to high-flying Newcastle United. On a sun-drenched pitch West Ham were in superb form winning 5-0. Winger Johnny Sissons scored twice but the Hammers' hero was young Brooking who scored a hat-trick.

WEDNESDAY 7TH APRIL 1965

Top Spanish side Real Zaragoza arrived at Upton Park for the first-leg of the semi-final in the European Cup Winners' Cup. The 35,000 or so fans inside Upton Park were delighted when Johnny Byrne and Brian Dear both scored within 25 minutes of the start of the game, but in the second half, the Spaniards pulled a goal back to leave the tie in the balance going into the second-leg in Spain three weeks later.

SATURDAY 7TH APRIL 2007

Fighting relegation the Hammers faced Arsenal at their new Emirates Stadium. A 60,098 crowd saw an inspired performance from Robert Green in the West Ham goal, as Bobby Zamora scored the only goal of the game. It gave West Ham renewed hope in the battle to avoid the drop and meant they became the first team to win at Arsenal's new home.

FRIDAY 8TH APRIL 1966

Good Friday and a local derby at White Hart Lane was watched by 50,365. Spurs took the lead after 15 minutes but the Hammers scored two goals in two first-half minutes through Johnny Byrne and Geoff Hurst. There was further joy for West Ham in the second half when two more goals came from Harry Redknapp and Ronnie Boyce. A good win – but the next day they conceded six at Chelsea...

SATURDAY 8TH APRIL 1978

The Hammers were embroiled in a struggle against relegation – and at Leeds United were 1-0 down after 25 minutes. A minute before half-time, new boy Alvin Martin equalised. Derek Hales scored after the break. Leeds missed a penalty, as West Ham held on for a 2-1 win.

SATURDAY 8TH APRIL 1987

A home First Division match against Arsenal which saw two early penalties for both sides. Tony Cottee scored for the Hammers and Martin Hayes for Arsenal. After the interval Cottee put West Ham ahead and then former Gunner Liam Brady added another for a fine 3-1 win.

SATURDAY 9TH APRIL 1966

After beating Spurs the day before, West Ham made seven changes for their visit to Chelsea. A rather disjointed side played poorly and Chelsea were leading 6-0 by the 80th minute. The Hammers made a slight rally by scoring twice through Peter Bennett and an own-goal.

FRIDAY 9TH APRIL 1971

A Good Friday First Division match at Upton Park with West Bromwich Albion, who had not won away for 16 months but took the lead in the first half to lead at half-time. The Hammers were rescued in the second half when Pop Robson equalised and Jimmy Greaves scored the winner.

WEDNESDAY 9TH APRIL 1975

Ipswich Town and West Ham meet in the FA Cup Semi-Final replay at Stamford Bridge. The Hammers triumphed, but the men from Suffolk felt hard done by as they had two goals disallowed. The hero for West Ham was Alan Taylor who scored twice as the Hammers marched on to Wembley, winning 2-1.

WEDNESDAY 10TH APRIL 1929

A meagre crowd of just 7,996 fans at Goodison Park for the First Division clash between Everton and West Ham. Both teams had suffered poor seasons and were languishing in the league – but it was a good day for the Hammers as they triumphed 4-0. Amateur forward Viv Gibbins scored his first hat-trick for the club; an own-goal completed the scoring.

SATURDAY 10TH APRIL 1937

The Hammers were bidding for promotion to the First Division as they welcomed lowly Bradford City to Upton Park. A home crowd of 15,802 were delighted as they saw an emphatic 4-1 win for West Ham. Leading marksman Len Goulden was one of the scorers, while Joe Foxall and Sammy Small (two) also netted.

SATURDAY 11TH APRIL 1981

Promotion favourites West Ham travelled to Grimsby Town for this Second Division fixture. The Mariners had only conceded four goals at home all season, but their impressive record was shattered as the magical Hammers won 5-1 with striker David Cross claiming four of the goals. Geoff Pike was the other scorer as the Hammers stayed on course for promotion and kept their place at the top of the league.

SATURDAY 11TH APRIL 1992

The Hammers were bottom of the First Division and had not won for nine games. For the visit of Norwich City, 20-year-old Matthew Rush was brought into the side. The youngster celebrated with two fine goals and the whole team responded, winning 4-0. Julian Dicks netted a penalty with Ian Bishop getting the other goal. It was an impressive victory, but would it help the Hammers avoid the drop ahead of the formation of the new Premier League...

SATURDAY 12TH APRIL 1941

Bobby Moore was born in Barking, Essex. Arguably the best defender in the world he became a Hammers legend. At youth level he won 18 caps for England and then progressed to the England Under-23 team, winning eight caps before going on to make 108 full international appearances. Moore lifted three trophies at Wembley Stadium in three consecutive seasons; with West Ham he won the FA Cup in 1964; a year later, the European Cup Winners' Cup; finally, famously, and unforgettably he was captain of the victorious England team that won the World Cup in 1966. In an illustrious West Ham career he played in a total of 642 League and Cup games, scoring 27 goals. He moved on to Fulham in 1974 and was in the Fulham team that played West Ham in the 1975 FA Cup Final. With the Cottagers, he played a further 150 games before retiring in May 1977. He later managed Oxford City and Southend United. The world of football was shattered when he sadly died in February 1993.

FRIDAY 12TH APRIL 1974

A relegation battle at Upton Park as the Hammers faced Southampton. The Saints went ahead with a penalty but Pop Robson equalised. In the second half West Ham took control with another goal from Robson. There were also two goals from Clyde Best in the 4-1 victory.

SATURDAY 12TH APRIL 2003

Fighting the drop from the Premiership, West Ham drew 2-2 with Aston Villa, with Fredi Kanoute and Trevor Sinclair on target. An Upton Park crowd of 35,029 saw the Hammers miss chances as two points were lost.

FRIDAY 13TH APRIL 1956

Park Royal in London was the birthplace of Alan Devonshire. He was spotted playing in non-league football with Southall and joined West Ham for the bargain fee of £5,000 in 1976. Alan was a joy to watch and became one of the most skilful players in the club's history. He set up a brilliant midfield partnership with Trevor Brooking which was hugely successful when West Ham won the FA Cup in 1980. International recognition followed as he gained eight England caps. After 15 years' great service he left in 1990 to join Watford for a short period. In his time with the Hammers, Alan played in a total of 447 league and cup games, scoring 32 goals.

SATURDAY 13TH APRIL 1963

High-flying Leicester City came to Upton Park as league leaders and unbeaten in 16 games. Having lost at home the previous day to Ipswich the Hammers needed to put on a good performance and centre-forward Alan Sealey scored a goal in each half to give West Ham a 2-0 victory.

SATURDAY 13TH APRIL 2002

Both West Ham and Tottenham were in the top ten when they met at White Hart Lane. The home side went ahead in the second half when Teddy Sheringham – who later joined West Ham – put Spurs ahead, but with just a minute remaining, defender Ian Pearce equalised with a stunning volley, on his 100th club appearance.

WEDNESDAY 14TH APRIL 1976

A big European night at Upton Park as Eintracht Frankfurt were the opponents in the Cup Winners Cup semi-final second-leg. Trailing 2-1 from the first-leg, the Hammers equalised just after half-time with a goal from Trevor Brooking. Another goal from Brooking (a rare header) was followed by a 30-yard curler from Keith Robson. The Germans pulled a goal back late in the game but it was West Ham who progressed.

SATURDAY 14TH APRIL 1991

West Ham and Nottingham Forest met in the semi-final of the FA Cup at Villa Park. After 26 minutes Tony Gale was controversially sent off after what looked an innocuous foul. However, it remained a balanced game until half-time, but in the second half, Forest were well on top scoring four without reply. Forest full-backs Stuart Pearce and Gary Charles scored two of the goals, and both men later joined West Ham. The match will be remembered by Hammers' fans present for their non-stop singing of "Billy Bonds Claret and Blue Army" during the second half.

SATURDAY 15TH APRIL 1916

The first season of wartime football saw a supplementary tournament installed instead of the usual cup competition. The Hammers were undefeated at home when they entertained Reading, and the Berkshire side were overwhelmed as West Ham scored freely in a 7-0 victory. Danny Shea, Syd Puddefoot and Andrew Cunningham all scored twice with a further goal coming from Jack Casey.

FRIDAY 15TH APRIL 1960

Smarting from a 5-0 defeat at Wolverhampton four days previous West Ham faced Manchester United at Upton Park. Before kick-off the gates were locked with thousands outside. Those lucky enough to get in saw the Hammers score two goals within the first six minutes from their wingers, Mike Grice and Malcolm Musgrove. The Reds also scored in the first half but West Ham held on for a 2-1 victory.

THURSDAY 16TH APRIL 1953

The first-ever floodlit match at Upton Park took place with a friendly against Tottenham Hotspur. The Hammers team wore bright, fluorescent shirts. In a keenly-fought match West Ham won 2-1 with goals from Jim Barrett and Tommy Dixon.

FRIDAY 16TH APRIL 1965

A Good Friday home First Division fixture against West Bromwich Albion saw the Hammers romp to their biggest win of the season. After Martin Peters put West Ham in the lead, the match then belonged to striker Brian Dear. In a 20-minute spell he scored an amazing five goals and the Hammers eventually won 6-1.

WEDNESDAY 16TH APRIL 1980

A great night for the Hammers at Elland Road, as they faced Everton in an FA Cup semi-final replay. A 40,720 crowd witnessed the 2-1 win which put West Ham into the final. All the goals were scored in extra-time: the first coming from a solo run by Alan Devonshire. The winner came minutes from the end: a rare headed goal from Frank Lampard.

TUESDAY 16TH APRIL 2002

Michael Carrick and Jermain Defoe were both in the England under-21 side that lost 1-0 to Portugal at Stoke City's Britannia Stadium.

SATURDAY 17 APRIL 1964

After three successive First Division defeats, FA Cup finalists West Ham bounced back with a fine win. Playing at home against lowly Birmingham City, the Hammers scored five goals without reply. For the final home game of the season the crowd of 22,106 were treated to goals from Peter Brabrook (two), Johnny Byrne, Geoff Hurst and John Sissons.

SATURDAY 17TH APRIL 1999

Derby County and West Ham were both in the Premiership's top ten when they met at Upton Park, but County collapsed under the Hammers' onslaught as they ran out 5-1 winners. Paolo Di Canio scored a brilliant 20-yarder, with the others coming from Eyal Berkovic, Ian Wright, Neil Ruddock and Trevor Sinclair.

WEDNESDAY 17TH APRIL 2002

Playing for England against Paraguay at Liverpool were Joe Cole and Trevor Sinclair. The Hammers' duo both came on as second half substitutes during England's 4-0 friendly win.

TUESDAY 18TH APRIL 1961

West Ham faced a tough trip to Championship-chasing Burnley. The game looked lost as the home side took a 2-0 lead in the second half, but winger Malcolm Musgrove came to the Hammers' rescue with two late goals to level the scores.

SATURDAY 18TH APRIL 1981

Unbeaten in the last 12 league games, the Hammers made the short trip to play Orient in confident mood. Jimmy Neighbour burst through for the first goal and Geoff Pike hit a rocket shot for the second goal. The Hammers kept things tight in the second half and the game ended with a 2-0 victory to keep West Ham firmly in line for promotion.

SATURDAY 19TH APRIL 1958

A crucial Second Division game for both teams as West Ham entertained Liverpool. It was the final home game of the season and 37,734 fans crammed into Upton Park for this promotion clash. In a rousing encounter the Reds took the lead but West Ham equalised in the last quarter to share the spoils of a 1-1 draw, which would help the Hammers win the Second Division title.

SATURDAY 19TH APRIL 1986

The Hammers were in fifth place in the First Division and enjoying an excellent season. A trip to Watford saw the Hammers' strike duo of Tony Cottee and Frank McAvennie net a goal each in the second half to clinch a 2-0 victory.

SATURDAY 20th APRIL 1901

Playing at the Memorial Grounds, this was the first season the club was known as West Ham United. The final home game in the Southern League saw the Hammers at home to New Brompton. A crowd of around 2,000 were happy to see West Ham win 2-0, with George Ratcliffe and Frank Taylor the goalscorers.

SATURDAY 20th APRIL 1929

Having been thumped 6-0 at Derby County earlier in the season the Hammers were looking for revenge in the home fixture. Leading scorer Vic Watson scored twice but it ended 2-2, as the Rams hit back.

FRIDAY 20th APRIL 1962

A Good Friday home fixture with lowly Cardiff City who were fighting against relegation from the First Division. The Welshmen were despatched with ease; Johnny Byrne scored his first goal for the club with further goals coming from Ian Crawford, Alan Sealey and an own-goal.

SATURDAY 21st APRIL 1962

The 31,912 fans at Upton Park saw a thriller with London rivals Arsenal. The goals flowed as the teams fought out an exciting 3-3 draw. Hammers' goalkeeper Lawrie Leslie went off injured and John Lyall went in goal. The Hammers' goals came from Johnny Dick, Tony Scott and Bill Lansdowne. The injured Leslie – with his arm strapped up – came back to play on the wing and provided the cross for the late equaliser.

SATURDAY 21st APRIL 1973

Away to high-flying Derby County, Irish international Bertie Lutton scored his first West Ham goal in the 75th minute, but Derby equalised in the dying minutes with a disputed penalty kick.

MONDAY 21st APRIL 1986

None of the 24,734 Upton Park crowd will forget this match with Newcastle United, who were crushed 8-1. Alvin Martin scored an amazing hat-trick – with each of his goals being scored against a different Newcastle goalkeeper. The other scorers were Paul Goddard, Frank McAvennie, Ray Stewart, Neil Orr and an own-goal from Glenn Roeder, who later became the Hammers' boss.

ALVIN MARTIN

WEDNESDAY 22ND APRIL 1942

Canning Town was the birthplace of goalscorer Alan Sealey. He started his career with Leyton Orient and then joined West Ham in 1961. He spent seven seasons at the club, playing in a total of 128 games and scoring 26 goals. Alan's finest moment came in May 1965 when he scored two goals at Wembley when the Hammers beat TSV Munich 2-0 to win the European Cup Winners' Cup. He later had short spells with Plymouth Argyle and Romford. He sadly died in 1996.

SATURDAY 22ND APRIL 1989

West Ham were having a miserable season and were bottom of the First Division. Playing at home to fierce rivals Millwall they needed a boost to excite the fans. In an exciting first half the Hammers scored three goals through Julian Dicks, George Parris and Alan Dickens. There was no further scoring and West Ham were good value for the 3-0 victory.

SATURDAY 22ND APRIL 2000

Coventry City arrived at Upton Park having not won away from Highfield Road for over a year. The Hammers were inspired by Paolo Di Canio who was in sparkling form and had a hand in all the goals in a thumping 5-0 victory. As well as setting up goals for Michael Carrick, Javier Margas and Fredi Kanoute, talented Italian Di Canio also scored two himself.

MONDAY 23RD APRIL 1962

Having beaten Cardiff City 4-1 on the Good Friday, the Hammers travelled to Wales for the return fixture on Easter Monday. The Bluebirds were at the foot of the table but easily won this game 3-0. It was a disappointing day for West Ham as goalkeeper Brian Rhodes went off injured and Martin Peters played in goal for the remaining half hour.

SATURDAY 23RD APRIL 2005

The Hammers were looking to figure in the Championship play-offs when they faced Brighton & Hove Albion at Withdean. It was Nigel Reo-Coker who scored first after eight minutes, but Albion levelled on 53 minutes. Two minutes later West Ham took the lead through Marlon Harewood and looked the likely winners, but Hammers' fans were left disappointed when Albion equalised in the last minute to draw 2-2.

SATURDAY 24TH APRIL 1920

This was the first season that West Ham had played in the Football League. A home game with Hull City drew an attendance of 18,000 to Upton Park. A 2-1 win meant the Hammers had won five successive home games. The West Ham scorers on this occasion were Syd Puddefoot and Dan Bailey.

SATURDAY 24TH APRIL 1982

A seven-goal thriller excited a crowd of 24,748 at Upton Park. Lowly Leeds United were the visitors and needed the points to help them in their battle against relegation. They were winning 1-0 at half-time but the second half brought goals galore and by the final whistle the Hammers had won 4-3. Two goals came from Trevor Brooking and one apiece were scored by David Cross and Ray Stewart.

SATURDAY 24TH APRIL 1993

The season was reaching an exciting climax as the Hammers pressed for promotion to the Premier League. Visitors Bristol Rovers who were bottom of the league had already been relegated, so it was a surprise when the Pirates took the lead in the second half – but West Ham fought back. First Julian Dicks scored from a penalty then David Speedie scored the winner from a header.

SATURDAY 25TH APRIL 1964

The season ended with an away game at Everton, who were in third position in the First Division. Mindful of the forthcoming FA Cup Final, the Hammers rested striker Johnny Byrne and skipper Bobby Moore. The game was a typical end-of-season contest and a goal in each half gave the Blues a 2-0 win.

SATURDAY 25TH APRIL 1978

The final away game of the season saw the Hammers travel to Middlesbrough. They were in serious trouble third from bottom in the table and nothing less than a win would do. When the home side took the lead on 17 minutes it looked very bleak for the Hammers. However, David Cross later scored from a header and in a goalmouth scramble netted the winner, but would it be enough to help West Ham avoid the drop from the First Division...

SATURDAY 26TH APRIL 1947

Barnsley were at Upton Park for a Second Division fixture. The 16,275 crowd witnessed West Ham romp home 4-0. Both wingers – Terry Woodgate and Ken Bainbridge – were on the scoresheet with leading scorer Eric Parsons grabbing two more.

SATURDAY 26TH APRIL 1952

Sheffield Wednesday had just clinched the Second Division title when they welcomed West Ham to Hillsborough for the final game of the season. A massive crowd of 44,051 turned up to see their favourites. The Owls had already won 6-0 at Upton Park earlier in the season so the Hammers faced a daunting task – but they fared better as goals from Jim Barrett and Gerry Gazzard gave them a creditable 2-2 draw.

SATURDAY 26TH APRIL 1958

League leaders West Ham made the trip to Middlesbrough, needing a win to be promoted to the First Division. There were 30,526 inside Ayresome Park and West Ham faced the threat of 40-goal Brian Clough. However, the Hammers had their own goal power in John Dick and Vic Keeble. They both scored, along with Malcom Musgrove, for a deserved 3-1 victory which clinched the Second Division Championship.

SATURDAY 27TH APRIL 1929

The long journey to Sunderland for West Ham's final away game of the season. The Wearside club were fourth in the league with their top scorer Dave Halliday having 40 goals to his name. West Ham's own leading man Vic Watson, however, brought his total of the season to 20 by scoring the first goal in front of a meagre crowd of 9,469. But Sunderland replied with four goals: star man Halliday claimed three of them.

SATURDAY 27TH APRIL 1971

For the final away game of the campaign, the Hammers were at The Dell to face Southampton. West Ham were one place above the two already relegated clubs. With the Saints pressing for a place in Europe, it was against the formbook that Tommy Taylor scored his first goal for the club to put the Hammers ahead. Another goal from Geoff Hurst in the second half put the Londoners in control, and although Southampton scored late in the game the Hammers held on to win 2-1.

SATURDAY 28TH APRIL 1923

A famous day in the history of English football as the first-ever FA Cup Final was staged at the new Wembley Stadium. The participants were Second Division West Ham United and First Division Bolton Wanderers. There was total chaos before the game as thousands climbed in over the gates and spilled on to the pitch, and although the fans were cleared from the pitch to start the game, they still stood all along the touchline throughout the contest which especially hindered West Ham's wingers. Bolton were the better side, winning 2-0. The official attendance was given as 126,047 but it was believed to be far higher.

WEDNESDAY 28TH APRIL 1965

The Hammers faced a daunting task in Spain against Spanish Cup Winners Real Zaragoza. It was the second-leg of the European Cup Winners' Cup semi-final, and West Ham were leading 2-1 from the first-leg at Upton Park – but the Spaniards levelled the tie after 24 minutes, and West Ham now had to score. Led by skipper Bobby Moore, West Ham defended brilliantly and it was young Johnny Sissons in the second half who grabbed an equaliser. The game ended 1-1 to ensure West Ham a place in the Wembley final where they would meet TSV Munich.

WEDNESDAY 28TH APRIL 1999

Rio Ferdinand was in the England team for their friendly international with Hungary in Budapest, where the teams drew 1-1.

SATURDAY 28TH APRIL 2007

West Ham were attempting the great escape to avoid relegation from the Premiership; a few weeks earlier they had looked dead and buried. Over 9,000 Hammers' fans made the trip to fellow strugglers Wigan. West Ham had won at the JJB Stadium in the four previous seasons and this run continued with an emphatic 3-0 victory. Luis Boa Morte, Yossi Benayoun and Marlon Harewood were the scorers.

SATURDAY 29TH APRIL 1946

The last home game in the Football League South competition, introduced after the war. West Ham were at home to Fulham and were unbeaten in eight games. In a season of high scoring matches West Ham went down 5-3. Almeric Hall (two) and Jackie Wood got the goals.

SATURDAY 29TH APRIL 2005

Teddy Sheringham was named Hammer of the Year for 2004/05. The veteran striker was leading scorer that season with 20 league goals. His goals and presence went a long way in helping West Ham to qualify for the play-offs and subsequently gain promotion to the Premiership.

MONDAY 30TH APRIL 1986

West Ham attracted a gate of 31,121, their biggest of the season, for the last home game of the season against Ipswich Town. The Hammers could still win the title, so it was a shock when Ipswich took the lead in the second half but Alan Dickens equalised soon after, and with four minutes remaining there was more drama as West Ham were awarded a penalty. Ice-cool Ray Stewart stepped up to blast the ball into the net for a last-gasp 2-1 victory.

SATURDAY 30TH APRIL 1994

After suffering two home Premier League defeats, West Ham made the trip across London to face the Arsenal. It was stalemate at half-time but in the second half it was the Hammers who came out on top, scoring twice without reply. Trevor Morley got the first and Martin Allen netted the other, his fourth goal in four games. It was the Gunners' first league defeat in 20 games.

SUNDAY 30TH APRIL 1995

League leaders Blackburn Rovers arrived at Upton Park keen to extend their lead at the top of the Premiership, and it was not looking good for the Hammers when top scorer Tony Cottee failed a late fitness test. However, second half goals from Marc Rieper and Don Hutchison gave West Ham a deserved 2-0 victory.

WEST HAM UNITED
On This Day

MAY

SATURDAY 1st MAY 1920

West Ham completed their first season in the Football League with a home game against Stockport County. It was a successful first campaign and this game ended 3-0 in the Hammers' favour. Leading scorer Syd Puddefoot netted one goal, with the others coming from Syd Butcher and skipper George Kay.

SATURDAY 1st MAY 1999

An amazing turn of events in the home game with Leeds United, with three West Ham players sent off by referee Rob Harris. Taking an early bath were Steve Lomas, Shaka Hislop and Ian Wright. As for the football, Paolo Di Canio scored for the Hammers, but Leeds scored five to make it an unhappy day for most of the 25,997 present.

SATURDAY 2nd MAY 1964

A proud day in the history of the club as West Ham won the FA Cup for the very first time. Playing against Second Division Preston North End, the Lancashire team twice took the lead but were thwarted by equalisers from John Sissons and Geoff Hurst; and in the dying minute there was a dramatic finish to the game as Ronnie Boyce headed the winner from a Peter Brabrook cross. It was a proud Bobby Moore who collected the trophy as 'I'm Forever Blowing Bubbles' drifted around the stadium.

SATURDAY 2nd MAY 1981

Already Second Division champions West Ham went into the home game with Wrexham unbeaten in the previous 15 league games. The game was an anti-climax – the Hammers won 1-0 with a penalty from Ray Stewart – but at the final whistle 30,515 fans saluted their heroes and looked forward to returning to the First Division.

SATURDAY 2nd MAY 1992

The Hammers were already relegated when they met Nottingham Forest at Upton Park on the season's final day. It was a dull first half and the interval arrived with the score at 0-0 – but things changed when Frank McAvennie came on as a substitute. Playing in his last game for the club, McAvennie bowed out in a suitable manner, scoring a hat-trick within a 25-minute spell. The 3-0 victory was a fitting end to the West Ham career of the much-loved Scottish international.

SATURDAY 3RD MAY 1941

Brentford were at Upton Park for a wartime league clash. The Hammers included regulars such as Ernie Gregory, Dick Walker and Len Goulden. The crowd of around 3,000 witnessed a 3-2 win, with goals from Sam Small, George Foreman and Harold Hobbis.

SATURDAY 3RD MAY 1975

West Ham were up against legend and former skipper Bobby Moore as they met Fulham in the FA Cup Final at Wembley. The Cottagers were on top in the early stages forcing Hammers' keeper Mervyn Day into two fine saves. It was all-square at half-time, but the second half belonged to Alan Taylor. He had scored twice in the semi-final and repeated this as Fulham's keeper made errors on both occasions. So the game, dubbed the Cockney Cup Final, was won by the happy Hammers with Billy Bonds collecting the trophy.

THURSDAY 4TH MAY 1933

The Upton Park district was the birthplace of tough tackling wing-half Andy Malcolm. He played for England Schoolboys and was the club's first-ever England youth international. He made his debut in December 1953 and went on to play in a total of 306 league and cup matches until he joined Chelsea in 1962. He later had a spell at Queens Park Rangers before emmigrating to South Africa, where he still lives.

SATURDAY 4TH MAY 1985

A sparse attendance of 8,834 at the Hawthorns see West Bromwich Albion beat West Ham 5-1. Ray Stewart gets the goal.

WEDNESDAY 5TH MAY 1976

The European Cup Winners' Cup Final at Heysel Stadium, Brussels, with West Ham facing Anderlecht, on home soil. A good start for the Hammers saw Pat Holland score after 28 minutes, but just before half-time Frank Lampard misjudged a back pass and the Belgians equalised. Anderlecht scored again just after half-time, but the Hammers hit back when Trevor Brooking set up Keith Robson to level at 2-2. In the 76th minute Anderlecht scored from a penalty. Two minutes from time François Van Der Elst raced through the West Ham defence to make it 4-2. Five years later, Van Der Elst became a West Ham player.

TUESDAY 5TH MAY 1998

Chasing a UEFA Cup place, West Ham were expected to win at bottom club Crystal Palace – especially after being gifted an own-goal in the fourth minute. However, the Eagles came back with three goals. With top scorer John Hartson suspended, the Hammers fielded young Manny Omoyinmi who responded by netting two late goals to square the game at 3-3.

SATURDAY 5TH MAY 2007

A vital must-win home game with Bolton Wanderers, as the Hammers were battling against the drop. In the first half-hour of the match, West Ham were unstoppable. Carlos Tevez scored with a 20-yard free-kick after ten minutes and doubled the advantage when, on 21 minutes, he crashed a second past the Bolton keeper. After 29 minutes he was the provider when his cross was volleyed home by Mark Noble. Bolton scored a consolation in the second half but the 3-1 win enabled West Ham to climb out of the bottom three.

SATURDAY 6TH MAY 1922

West Ham travelled to Blackpool for the final game of the campaign. In front of 12,000 fans, the Hammers lost 3-1. Making his debut in the West Ham team was 17-year-old Billy Williams who scored the Hammers' goal – and became the youngest ever Hammer.

SATURDAY 6TH MAY 1939

The final home game of the season and Manchester City were at Upton Park for a Second Division fixture. West Ham won 2-1, completing a double over City. Cliff Hubbard, making his debut, scored one of the goals in a game which turned out to be his only appearance for the club. The other scorer was inside forward Len Goulden.

SATURDAY 7TH MAY 1994

A crowd of 26,952 were at Upton Park for a Premier League match with Southampton on the final day of the season – and the last which supporters were able to watch from the terraces at Upton Park. With a minute remaining, Saints were leading 3-2, but defender Ken Monkou headed into his own net to level the scores. Martin Allen and Danny Williamson were the other two scorers.

TUESDAY 7TH MAY 1996

To celebrate the club's centenary, a home friendly with Sporting Lisbon was arranged – but the Portuguese were too good for West Ham and won 4-1 with ease. Julian Dicks scored the goal with a 30-yarder.

SUNDAY 7TH MAY 2006

London rivals Tottenham provided the opposition at Upton Park for the final league game of the season. Before the game several of the Spurs players fell ill with food poisoning, but they got very little sympathy from the Hammers. Carl Fletcher put the Hammers ahead when he cracked in a 20-yarder after ten minutes, only for former West Ham striker Jermain Defoe to equalise on 35 minutes. There was second half drama as Teddy Sheringham missed a penalty against his old club, but the place erupted ten minutes from time when Yossi Benayoun scored the winner.

SATURDAY 8TH MAY 1993

It was tense inside Upton Park on the final day of the season, for a vital game against Cambridge United. West Ham had to win to be promoted and Cambridge had to win to stay up. It was a tense first half and at the interval it was 0-0. Two minutes into the second half David Speedie scored for the Hammers and, in the last minute, Clive Allen added a second for the game to end 2-0. The Hammers were promoted and the party started as thousands ran onto the pitch.

SATURDAY 8TH MAY 1999

The away game at Everton provided the Hammers with the chance to get back on track following the 5-1 home defeat the previous week to Leeds. This, however, turned out to be another disaster as the Merseysiders were convincing 6-0 winners. After conceding 11 goals in two games, goalkeeper Shaka Hislop was 'rested' the following week.

TUESDAY 9TH MAY 1989

West Ham were at Sheffield Wednesday for the first game at Hillsborough since the disaster which tragically killed 96 Liverpool supporters. Alan Dickens scored a good goal for the Hammers in the second half and a second arrived following a header from Leroy Rosenior. A 2-0 victory gave West Ham some hope of staying up but, sadly, they were relegated after the final game of the season.

WEDNESDAY 9TH MAY 2001

Shockwaves swept through the football world as it was announced that manager Harry Redknapp and his assistant Frank Lampard had parted company with the club. The club were in a disappointing 15th place in the league and had underachieved. Nonetheless Redknapp, a friendly, likeable man was a popular manager. He was boss for seven seasons.

SATURDAY 9TH MAY 2004

Wigan and West Ham met at the JJB stadium for a vital end-of-season clash that would affect the play-off places. Wigan needed to win the game to qualify for the play-offs. They went ahead after 34 minutes and held the lead until the last minute, when a cross from Michael Carrick was headed home by Brian Deane, leaving the home fans in despair as they realised the play-offs were beyond them.

SATURDAY 10TH MAY 1980

Second Division West Ham were the underdogs as they faced the mighty Arsenal in the FA Cup Final. On a scorching day the Hammers took a shock lead in the 13th minute when Trevor Brooking scored with a rare header. After that the West Ham defenders Billy Bonds and Alvin Martin were outstanding against the Gunners' attack. Arsenal became frustrated and the cup came back to the East End following this famous 1-0 victory.

SATURDAY 10TH MAY 1998

Prior to the home game with Leicester City Rio Ferdinand was named Hammer of the Year. The young defender had an outstanding season and was tipped to become a fixture in the England team for years to come – indeed he was named in the 1998 World Cup squad. The 25,781 fans welcomed back Tony Cottee – he came on as a substitute for Leicester – but they were not pleased when he scored two goals. The Hammers, however, were on top throughout with Samassi Abou scoring twice and Frank Lampard and Trevor Sinclair got a goal each in a 4-3 win.

SATURDAY 11TH MAY 1963

Already-down, Leyton Orient came to Upton Park. Peter Brabrook scored with a header in the first half and an overhead kick from Tony Scott gave West Ham a 2-0 win, in front of a 16,745 crowd.

WEDNESDAY 11TH MAY 1966

Long serving full-back John Bond was granted a Testimonial match against an Ex-Hammers XI. A crowd of around 10,000 were treated to a goal fest as West Ham won the game 7-4. In the Ex-Hammers side were former favourites Phil Woosnam, Ken Brown and Malcolm Musgrove. Among the West Ham scorers were Bobby Moore, Geoff Hurst and Martin Peters. Two months later they would all be playing in the World Cup Final.

SUNDAY 11TH MAY 2003

West Ham travelled to Birmingham City level on points with Bolton Wanderers at the foot of the table. The Hammers had been in fine form having won their three previous matches under the leadership of caretaker manager Trevor Brooking. All was going well when Rio Ferdinand headed West Ham ahead but the Blues then scored twice, and then at the end Paolo Di Canio equalised to make it 2-2. Unfortunately, at the final whistle, the news filtered through to the team and fans that Bolton had won, which left the Hammers relegated.

SATURDAY 12TH MAY 1945

Unlike many clubs during wartime football, the Hammers had been able to field a fairly settled side in 1944/45, and going into the penultimate game of the campaign, they were in second spot in the League South. Luton Town were the visitors and they were hammered 9-1 at Upton Park. Scorers in the goal spree were Almeric Hall (three), Charlie Whitchurch (three), Tom Cheetham (two) and Norman Corbett.

MONDAY 12TH MAY 1980

Two days after winning the FA Cup the Hammers had to face an electric atmosphere at Sunderland as the Wearsiders had to win the match to be promoted to the First Division. A massive crowd of 47,129 saw Sunderland win 2-0. The Hammers finished the game with ten men due to injuries.

FRIDAY 12TH MAY 2000

Frank Lampard and Michael Carrick are named in the England under-21 squad for the forthcoming European Championship finals in Slovakia.

SATURDAY 13TH MAY 2006

West Ham and Liverpool produced the best FA Cup Final for many years as they drew 3-3 at the Millennium Stadium. The Hammers took a two-goal lead thanks to an own-goal in the 20th minute from Jamie Carragher and a Dean Ashton goal after 28 minutes. Four minutes later the Reds were back in the game as Djibril Cisse fired home and nine minutes into the second half Liverpool were level when Steve Gerrard scored. West Ham kept going and Paul Konchesky scored a third with a cross-shot which sailed into the net – but with just a minute remaining the Hammers' hearts were broken when Gerrard equalised with a wonder shot from 30 yards. In extra-time, Reo-Coker hit the post and after the additional 30 minutes it finished 3-3. Liverpool won 3-1 on penalties with Teddy Sheringham the lone Hammers' shoot-out scorer.

SUNDAY 13TH MAY 2007

At the start of March 2007 the Hammers seemed to be facing certain relegation as they languished at the foot of the table. Then, a remarkable recovery – they won six games out of eight – gave them a chance of staying up. The last game of the season was a difficult trip to Old Trafford where they would play champions Manchester United. An amazing day for the 9,000 West Ham supporters when the Hammers won 1-0 courtesy of a goal from the brilliant Carlos Tevez, which meant the season will forever be remembered as 'The Great Escape'.

MONDAY 14TH MAY 1984

The final game of the campaign against Everton and the Hammers lost 1-0. The result didn't matter much: the fans were there to bid farewell to a retiring Trevor Brooking. The England international played 634 games for West Ham, scoring 102 goals. The fans stayed at the end to applaud Brooking as he completed a well-deserved lap of honour.

SUNDAY 14TH MAY 1995

A vital game for Manchester United at West Ham; they needed to win to have any chance of pipping Blackburn to the title. Michael Hughes made it 1-0 after half an hour; United equalised after 52 minutes and then mounted wave after wave of attacks. But Ludek Miklosko had his finest game for the club, making save after save to keep the scores level at 1-1, to the delight of West Ham and Blackburn fans.

THURSDAY 14TH MAY 1998

Frank Lampard was in the England under-21 team for their friendly against France in Toulon. He skippered the side to a 1-1 draw.

MONDAY 15TH MAY 1967

A well-deserved testimonial game for stalwart Ken Brown. The Hammers played a Select XI before a crowd of 14,695, who saw a goal bonanza as the Select XI won 9-5. Brown played for the Select XI alongside stars such as Gordon Banks, Rodney Marsh and George Eastham. Scorers for West Ham were Dave Bickles, Bobby Moore, Geoff Hurst, Colin Mackleworth and an own-goal.

SATURDAY 15TH MAY 1982

There were only 13,283 spectators at Molineux for the game against Wolverhampton Wanderers. It was a poor start for the Hammers as they were two down after ten minutes. David Cross pulled a goal back but it was Wolves who finished 2-1 winners – but were still relegated.

SATURDAY 16TH MAY 1977

West Ham went into the home game with Manchester United having lost only once in the last 12 league games. United scored within a minute of the start but Frank Lampard equalised before half-time. The game was sealed after the interval as Pop Robson scored twice and – after United pulled one back – a further goal came from Geoff Pike. leaving the 29,311 home faithful pleased with a 4-2 victory.

SUNDAY 16TH MAY 1999

Middlesbrough were beaten 4-0 at Upton Park. Frank Lampard put the Hammers ahead after four minutes, and after that the outcome was never in doubt. Marc Keller added to the score before half-time and Trevor Sinclair wrapped the game up with two goals after the break.

FRIDAY 16TH MAY 2003

The club issued a statement saying that following relegation there needed to be financial cutbacks which would result in the release of the following eight players: Lee Bowyer, Gary Breen, Edouard Cisse, Paolo Di Canio, Scott Minto, John Moncur, Raimond Van Der Gouw and Nigel Winterburn.

SATURDAY 17TH MAY 1941

The London War Cup was run on a league basis until the semi-finals. West Ham were playing away to Arsenal in the final league game where they lost 3-0. Only six wins out of ten matches was not enough to proceed further.

FRIDAY 17TH MAY 1985

For the final away game of the season West Ham were at Portman Road to play Ipswich Town. An attendance of 19,278 saw Tony Cottee score the only goal of the game and secure a vital win which secured West Ham's top-flight status – defeat would have meant relegation.

FRIDAY 17TH MAY 1996

The youth team faced a tough task as they travelled to Liverpool for the second-leg of the FA Youth Cup Final. Trailing 2-0 from the first-leg there was hope when Frank Lampard scored in the first minute but the Reds came back with two goals to win 4-1 on aggregate.

SATURDAY 18TH MAY 1963

Manchester City came to Upton Park needing a win to avoid relegation. All hope was lost when Geoff Hurst scored twice in the first eight minutes. It turned out to be a massacre as Alan Sealey, with two, Ronnie Boyce and Peter Brabrook all got on the scoresheet. City did get a consolation goal but a 6-1 defeat sent them into the Second Division.

THURSDAY 18TH MAY 1989

The Hammers scored the fastest goal of the season, after just 19 seconds! They were away to Nottingham Forest when a cross from Liam Brady was put away by Leroy Rosenior. He also scored again after 18 minutes as the Hammers fought against relegation. Forest pulled a goal back but West Ham won 2-1, their fifth victory in six games.

TUESDAY 18TH MAY 2004

An incredible night of drama and passion at Upton Park as West Ham faced Ipswich Town in the second-leg of the play-off semi-final. The Hammers were 1-0 down, but spurred on by the fans, they scored two second half goals to win the tie. Matty Etherington opened the scoring and Christian Dailly added a second 20 minutes from time.

WEDNESDAY 19TH MAY 1965

One of the finest ever games seen at Wembley Stadium. The European Cup Winners' Cup Final paired West Ham with the German side TSV Munich. It was a magical night as Alan Sealey scored twice to give West Ham a 2-0 victory. Two sporting sides gave a wonderful exhibition of football that was admired around the world.

SATURDAY 19TH MAY 2012

West Ham overcame Blackpool at Wembley in the play-off final to return to the Premier League. A goal from Carlton Cole and one three minutes from time, by Ricardo Vaz Te, gave the Hammers a 2-1 victory which ensured promotion to the top flight of English football.

FRIDAY 20TH MAY 1898

Goalkeeper Tommy Hampson was born in Bury. He was signed from South Shields in 1920 and made his debut at Clapton Orient. He was understudy to the great Ted Hufton but, when Hufton suffered a serious knee injury in 1924, Tommy carried on with great authority. Before joining Blackburn Rovers in 1925, he played in a total of 79 league and cup games.

MONDAY 20TH MAY 1985

The final home game of the campaign was a First Division match against Liverpool. Frank Lampard came into the side for his first game of the season – but it turned out to be his last for the club. Liverpool won the game 3-0 even though they had to play the last 26 minutes with ten men due to injury.

SUNDAY 21ST MAY 1995

The Hammers were on tour in Australia, playing Victoria in Melbourne. The Aussies took the lead just before half-time and Danny Shipp headed a second half equaliser. Ian Feuer impressing in the Hammers' goal played before a crowd of 3,500 – made up of a lot of West Ham ex-pats who were keen to get a rare sight of the team in action.

TUESDAY 21ST MAY 2002

Trevor Sinclair and Joe Cole came on as half-time substitutes for England in the 1-1 draw against South Korea in Seoguipo.

WEDNESDAY 22ND MAY 1940

The Football League War Cup brought Huddersfield Town to Upton Park for a replay, following a 3-3 draw at Huddersfield. The season's biggest attendance of 20,000 turned up to see the Hammers win 3-1 to progress to Round Four. The scorers were Archie Macaulay, George Foreman and Joe Foxall.

THURSDAY 22ND MAY 2003

The West Ham trio of David James, Trevor Sinclair and Joe Cole all gained caps when playing for England in their 2-1 win against South Africa in Durban.

TUESDAY 23RD MAY 1989

A packed house at Anfield saw FA Cup winners Liverpool meet West Ham in the final game of the season. The Hammers needed to win the game to avoid relegation to the Second Division. It was 1-1 at half-time; Leroy Rosenior cancelling out the Reds' opener. After the break, however, Liverpool took control and added four further goals to complete a 5-1 romp and consign the Hammers to relegation.

SATURDAY 24TH MAY 1941

An exciting wartime game with Chelsea at Upton Park in the wartime Football League South. The 2,500 spectators were rewarded with a 3-3 draw. In goal for the Hammers was Syd Hobbins, a guest player from Charlton. Also playing as a guest was Berry Niewenhuys from Liverpool who scored two of the goals. The other scorer was winger Joe Foxall, who brought his tally up to 12 goals for the season.

SATURDAY 24TH MAY 1947

The Hammers faced a daunting task away to Second Division leaders Manchester City. The game attracted 33,771 spectators to Maine Road. West Ham were unbeaten in six games – but on this occasion lost 2-0.

WEDNESDAY 24TH MAY 1967

West Ham made the trip to the Republic of Ireland to play Shamrock Rovers. The Irish fans would have been pleased with the goal feast they witnessed as the teams drew 5-5. On the scoresheet for the Hammers were Geoff Hurst (two), John Sissons (two) and Brian Dear.

SUNDAY 25TH MAY 1969

The Hammers were on a tour of the United States where they played an exhibition match against Dundee United in Portland. The game was played on an artificial surface which must have been to West Ham's liking as they won 8-2. Grabbing the goals were Peter Bennett (two), Geoff Hurst (two), Martin Peters (two), Bobby Howe and Harry Redknapp.

FRIDAY 25TH MAY 2001

England beat Mexico 4-0 at Derby County's Pride Park. Michael Carrick and Joe Cole both made their full England debuts. The previous evening, Jermain Defoe scored on his England under-21 debut as the hosts beat Mexico 3-0 at Leicester City.

MONDAY 26TH MAY 1947

Newcastle wound down their Second Division league programme with a visit from the Hammers. There were 30,112 spectators inside St James' Park to see the Geordies lose 3-2. Their legendary scorers were Jackie Milburn and Len Shackleton, while the Hammers' goals came from Ken Bainbridge, Almeric Hall and Jackie Wood.

SUNDAY 26TH MAY 2002

An England friendly international with Cameroon in Kobe saw the teams draw 2-2. In the England side was Joe Cole and, coming on as second half substitutes, were Trevor Sinclair and David James.

TUESDAY 27TH MAY 1969

The Hammers were in America playing in an International Soccer League where each of the British teams was representing an American city. West Ham were representing Baltimore, where the game was played. They beat Aston Villa 2-0, with England international Martin Peters scoring both the goals.

SATURDAY 27TH MAY 1995

West Ham completed their tour of Australia by playing the Australian Under-23 team at Brisbane. The Hammers fielded a very inexperienced side as some first-teamers had already returned home to England. The decimated squad found it hard against the Aussies and slumped to a 4-0 defeat before 6,998 spectators.

TUESDAY 27 MAY 1997

Making his debut for Wales against Scotland at Kilmarnock was John Hartson. He scored the only goal of the match in the 46th minute.

TUESDAY 27TH MAY 2003

Midfielder Christian Dailly was in the Scotland team for their 1-1 friendly with New Zealand at Tynecastle Stadium, home of Hearts.

SUNDAY 28TH MAY 1893

Right-back Tommy Brandon was born in Blackburn and signed for West Ham in 1913 where he made his debut in September against Bristol Rovers in the Southern League. He went on to play in 33 league games before joining Hull City in 1920. He later played for Bradford and Wigan. Tommy died in May 1956.

SATURDAY 29TH MAY 1965

The Hammers' midfielder and captain Ian Bishop was born in Liverpool and has the distinction of playing in all four divisions of the Football League. He started as an apprentice at Everton in 1983 and was loaned out to Crewe Alexandra for four games in 1984. He then joined Carlisle United, playing in 132 league games before being transferred to Bournemouth in 1988. After 46 league games for the Cherries he went to Manchester City in 1989 where he played 19 league games in four months. It was manager Billy Bonds who signed him for West Ham in December 1989. Ian was a talented play-maker and went on to captain the club. He played until 1998, making a total of 299 league and cup appearances, before returning to Manchester City. He later played in America for Miami Fusion and for Barry Town in Wales, before ending his playing career at Rochdale.

SATURDAY 29TH MAY 2004

The Second Division Play-Off Final at the Millennium Stadium – with the opponents being Crystal Palace. West Ham were the favourites but, on the day, gave a disappointing performance when a late goal from Palace saw the Hammers beaten 1-0. It was a poor performance, lacking the passion shown by the Hammers' fans. Manager Alan Pardew stated the team would learn from this and come back stronger the next season in their quest to return to the Premiership.

FRIDAY 30TH MAY 1969

West Ham completed their last game in the American International League when they met Kilmarnock in Baltimore. After losing 2-1 to the Scots in Seattle, the Hammers got their revenge by winning this game 4-1. Scorers on this occasion were Boyce, Bennett, Hartley and Lindsay. It was an exhausting month-long tournament covering some 20,000 miles with half a dozen different airlines.

SATURDAY 30TH MAY 2005

After disappointment 12 months previously, The Hammers were back again in Cardiff for another crack at the Play-Off Final, this time against Preston North End. After the disappointment of the previous season, the team were in a confident and determined mood. All went well and the hero was Bobby Zamora who netted the all-important winning goal in the 57th minute. A 1-0 victory returned the club to the Premiership. A Play-Off Final can be a nervy, tense affair; but for the winners it's remembered as a trophy won and a great day out for the fans.

SATURDAY 31ST MAY 1941

An away game at Queens Park Rangers in the wartime Football League South. There were 2,000 inside Loftus Road to see George Foreman net a hat-trick during a 5-1 win. Other scorers were Joe Foxall and Len Goulden. Amazingly, during the war, Foreman scored a total of 154 league goals and a further 34 in various cup competitions.

SATURDAY 31ST MAY 1947

FA Cup Finalists Burnley drew an attendance of 20,198 to Upton Park for the final game of the season. The high-riding Clarets had enjoyed a good season but it was still very much a shock when they beat West Ham 5-0 to record their biggest win of the campaign.

WEST HAM UNITED
On This Day

JUNE

SATURDAY 1st JUNE 1940

The day of the Football League War Cup semi-final played at Stamford Bridge; West Ham were playing against their London rivals Fulham. In an amazing match, the Hammers went into a four-goal lead with goals from George Foreman, Len Goulden, Sam Small and an own-goal. But with just 25 minutes left for play the Cottagers staged a magnificent rally as they came back with three goals. It was an exciting finale as West Ham hung on to win 4-3 and reach the Cup Final at Wembley.

SUNDAY 1st JUNE 1969

The Hammers finished their exhausting month-long tour of the United States by playing an exhibition match against Southampton in Bermuda. West Ham were leading 2-0 with 12 minutes remaining but then conceded four goals as they tired in the final stages. Trevor Hartley and Clyde Best were the Hammers' scorers.

THURSDAY 1st JUNE 2000

Frank Lampard played in the England under-21 side that lost 2-0 to Slovakia in Bratislava.

MONDAY 2nd JUNE 1941

After winning at Millwall in October, the Hammers were looking to do the double over their London rivals in a wartime Football League South game. However, the Lions ran out 3-0 winners before a crowd of around 3,500.

MONDAY 2nd JUNE 1975

The town of Nancy in France was the birthplace of full back Sebastian Schemmel. He was signed from Metz in January 2001 and was an instant hit. In 2001/02, he was virtually ever present and his excellent performances resulted in him being named as Hammer of the Year. After making 63 league appearances he joined Portsmouth in 2003 and played in 18 games for them before returning to France.

WEDNESDAY 2nd JUNE 1982

Talented midfielder Alan Devonshire was in the starting line up for England when they drew 1-1 with Iceland in Rejkjavik.

MONDAY 3RD JUNE 1940

Visitors Millwall won 2-1 at Upton Park in a wartime Football League South game. The Hammers' lone goal was scored by George Foreman. West Ham fielded three guests from Arsenal – namely Ted Drake, Eddie Hapgood and Ernie Curtis.

TUESDAY 3RD JUNE 2003

Jermain Defoe was one of the England under-21 scorers in the 3-2 victory against Serbia at Hull. Defoe was joined in the side by second half substitutes Stephen Bywater and Glen Johnson. On the same day, Joe Cole scored for England against Serbia in the 2-1 victory at Leicester City's Walkers Stadium.

THURSDAY 4TH JUNE 1964

Both Bobby Moore and Johnny Byrne were in the England team that played Portugal in the Pacaembu Stadium in Sao Paulo, Brazil. In the searing heat and on a poor pitch the teams drew 1-1.

THURSDAY 5TH JUNE 1930

The Hammers were on a summer tour of Denmark where they met Copenhagen. There was a crowd of around 12,000 present to see both teams score inside the first minute of play. It was an exciting contest which finished 3-3. Goalscorers for the Hammers were Les Wilkins (two) and Walter Pollard.

WEDNESDAY 5TH JUNE 1963

West Ham were competing in the American Soccer League tournament and their second match took place in Chicago against the Italian team Mantova. The Hammers were losing 2-0 after five minutes but fought back to draw level with goals from Geoff Hurst and Alan Sealey. Late in the game they conceded two more goals to lose 4-2.

TUESDAY 5TH JUNE 2001

The England under-21 team lost 3-1 to Greece in Athens in a European Championship match. In the England side were four West Ham players. Michael Carrick was the goalscorer while the other West Ham played who featured in the game were Jermain Defoe, Stephen Bywater and Joe Cole.

SUNDAY 6TH JUNE 1926

The final game of the tour to Spain brought West Ham to Vigo where they played against the hometown team. There were some dubious refereeing decisions in this game in favour of Vigo. The teams were level at 2-2 with five minutes remaining when the Spanish team scored the winner from what was reported as an off-side position. The Hammers' scorers were Vic Watson and Jim Barrett.

WEDNESDAY 6TH JUNE 1962

The club were playing Nyasaland in the first match of their tour of Africa. Bobby Moore did not come on the trip as he was on World Cup duty with the England team in Chile. West Ham won the game 4-0 with goals from Johnny Dick (two), Johnny Byrne and Alan Sealey.

TUESDAY 6TH JUNE 1967

West Ham were invited to play HJK Helsinki to celebrate the 60th anniversary of the Finnish club. The 10,000-strong crowd were rewarded with nine goals as the Hammers won 6-3. Goalkeeper Bobby Ferguson, recently bought from Kilmarnock, made his debut. Brian Dear and Geoff Hurst each netted twice, Ron Boyce and Martin Peters were the other scorers.

SATURDAY 7TH JUNE 1941

The final home game in the Football League South saw Queens Park Rangers visit Upton Park. At centre-half for the Hammers was Bernard Joy – a guest player from Arsenal. The west London side returned home after winning 3-2. Goalscorers for West Ham were Sammy Small and George Foreman.

FRIDAY 7TH JUNE 2002

In the World Cup in Japan, England beat Argentina in Sapporo. Hammer Trevor Sinclair came on as a substitute in the 19th minute to earn his sixth international cap.

SATURDAY 7TH JUNE 2003

West Ham's Christian Dailly was part of the Scotland side which drew against Germany in a 1-1 draw in Glasgow during a European Championship qualifying group.

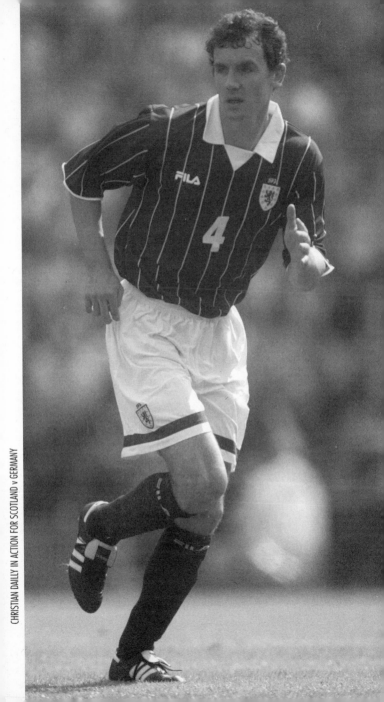

SATURDAY 8TH JUNE 1940

Wembley Stadium was the setting for the League War Cup Final between Blackburn Rovers and West Ham. The Hammers were the favourites and most of their attacks were coming from their wingers. In the 34th minute, Joe Foxall on the wing started a move before Len Goulden and George Foreman took it on. Foreman hit a shot which the goalkeeper could not hold and Small followed up to score. West Ham held on to win 1-0 and won a national trophy for the first time.

THURSDAY 8TH JUNE 1967

For the first game in their tour of Switzerland, West Ham played Grasshoppers in Zurich. The game was played in non-stop rain before a small attendance of around 2,000. The Hammers won 1-0 courtesy of a late goal from Harry Redknapp in a match which was also significant for the first team debut of Trevor Brooking.

WEDNESDAY 9TH JUNE 1875

The city of Edinburgh was the birthplace of Tommy Allison. After starting his career at New Brighton he then spent two seasons with Reading. He joined the Hammers in 1903 where he became a regular playing at half back. Tommy became the vice-captain and missed very few games until his last appearance in April 1909. In total, he played in 165 matches scoring seven goals.

TUESDAY 10TH JUNE 1930

The fourth game of the Scandinavian tour brought West Ham to Sweden where they played against Stockholm. The Swedish side were on top throughout and were worthy 4-0 winners in front of a crowd of 25,000.

SUNDAY 10TH JUNE 1962

Bobby Moore was in the England team beaten 3-1 by Brazil in the 1962 World Cup quarter-final. The game was played at Vina del Mar in Chile. Elsewhere, the rest of the West Ham team continued on their summer tour of South Africa, with a visit to play a Southern Rhodesia Select XI. It was an easy 5-0 victory for the Hammers with winger Malcolm Musgrove netting four goals. The other goal was scored by Johnny Byrne.

THURSDAY 11TH JUNE 1970

England played Czechoslovakia in the World Cup Finals in Mexico. Playing in the 1-0 victory was the Hammers duo of Bobby Moore and Martin Peters.

WEDNESDAY 11TH JUNE 2003

Playing in goal for England against Slovakia was David James. The game at Middlesbrough's Riverside Stadium was in the European Championship qualifiers and ended 2-1 in England's favour. Fellow Hammer Gary Breen was also playing in the same tournament. He was in the Republic of Ireland side that beat Georgia 2-0 in Dublin.

WEDNESDAY 12TH JUNE 1963

West Ham were playing their third game in the American Soccer League, against the Mexican side Oro. Bobby Moore and Johnny Byrne were in the side having missed the previous two matches as they were with the England squad. The Hammers won 3-1 with two goals from Geoff Hurst and another scored from a penalty taken by Byrne.

THURSDAY 12TH JUNE 1969

The Maracana Stadium was the scene for the friendly between Brazil and England. Bobby Moore was the England captain and playing alongside him were fellow West Ham team mates Geoff Hurst and Martin Peters.

WEDNESDAY 12TH JUNE 2002

Trevor Sinclair was in the England team that drew 0-0 with Nigeria in the World Cup Finals in Osaka, Japan.

SATURDAY 12TH JUNE 2004

In the Queen's Birthday Honours List, midfield maestro and ex-England star Trevor Brooking received a knighthood. Well done, Sir Trevor.

FRIDAY 13TH JUNE 1930

West Ham were on their tour of Sweden and faced Helsingborg, who claimed to be the best team in Scandinavia. It was a good game which finished 2-2 with the Hammers' goals coming from Charles Cox and Arthur Morris.

WEDNESDAY 13TH JUNE 1962

On tour in Africa, the Hammers played a return game with a Southern Rhodesia Select XI. They made five changes from the team that won 4-0 ten days previous. Brian Rhodes was in goal with the left-back now being John Lyall. It was another easy win, this time by 3-0, with Alan Sealey scoring twice. Malcolm Musgrove netted the other goal.

TUESDAY 13TH JUNE 1967

Continuing on their European tour, the Hammers played Lugano in Switzerland. An own-goal put the Swiss side ahead early in the game but West Ham fought back with goals from John Sissons and Brian Dear to lead 2-1 at the break. West Ham were on top in the second half, adding two more goals from Geoff Hurst and Peter Brabrook to win 4-1.

WEDNESDAY 14TH JUNE 1933

Harry Hooper was born in Pittingdon, County Durham. He came to West Ham in 1950 and, in six seasons, made a total of 130 League and Cup appearances, scoring 44 goals. The dashing outside right was a popular figure and there was uproar when he was sold to Wolverhampton Wanderers in 1956. After that he did not settle as he later joined Birmingham City and Sunderland – where he ended his career in 1963.

SUNDAY 14TH JUNE 1970

England were knocked out of the World Cup by West Germany in Leon, Mexico. Playing in the side were West Ham and England captain Bobby Moore, and fellow Hammer Geoff Hurst.

THURSDAY 14TH JUNE 2001

West Ham appointed Glenn Roeder as their ninth manager. It was a shock to the fans that the former reserve team coach would now be the manager. He did well in his first season, guiding the team to seventh place in the Premiership. The following season was a disaster for the team who were relegated and it was a personal tragedy for Roeder when, in April, he collapsed with a brain tumour. Fortunately he made a complete recovery and returned to his duties at the start of the 2003 season. After only three games into that campaign and, following a poor defeat at Rotherham, Roeder was sacked. He later became the manager at Newcastle United and Norwich City.

SATURDAY 15TH JUNE 2002

Trevor Sinclair, playing on the left, made an impressive impact as England beat Denmark 3-0 in the 2002 World Cup in Niigata.

THURSDAY 15TH JUNE 2006

Facing England in the World Cup Finals in Germany was Hammers goalkeeper Shaka Hislop. He was playing for Trinidad & Tobago and was on the losing side in the 2-0 defeat.

SATURDAY 16TH JUNE 2007

Veteran striker Teddy Sheringham was awarded an MBE for his services to football. He has enjoyed a glittering career winning many domestic and European medals and has gained 51 England caps. While with the Hammers, he scored 30 goals in 87 appearances.

WEDNESDAY 17TH JUNE 1908

Newcastle-upon-Tyne was the birthplace of George Robson. He made his debut for West Ham in his home city against Newcastle United in April 1928. His first-team opportunities were limited in his three seasons; he only made 17 league appearances, scoring two goals. He joined Brentford in 1931 where he won a Third Division Championship medal and, while there, scored 32 goals in 124 League appearances. He ended his playing career with Hearts before returning to West Ham to become a member of the scouting staff.

SUNDAY 17TH JUNE 1962

The Hammers were on a three-week tour to Africa. On this day they played the Hearts of Oak side from Ghana. The team continued with their unbeaten run by winning 4-1, with goals from Johnny Dick (two) and one apiece from Johnny Byrne and Ian Crawford.

FRIDAY 18TH JUNE 1965

Having won the American Soccer League in 1963, the Hammers returned to participate again. Their first game was against the New Yorkers and it was a poor start to the tournament. The Hammers gave away an own-goal then went 2-0 down in the 66th minute. There was hope when Ronnie Boyce reduced the deficit but the Americans ran out 2-1 winners.

SUNDAY 18TH JUNE 1967

The skilful Canadian international Alex Bunbury was born in British Guyana. It was a gamble by Billy Bonds to buy him in 1992 and he never reproduced his best form for West Ham. Playing one season, he only made five appearances and failed to score a goal. He was transferred to the Portuguese club Sporting Maritomo where he fared much better, scoring 59 goals in 165 league games. He was a popular player in Canada, having won 65 caps.

FRIDAY 19TH JUNE 1874

The Lincolnshire town of Gainsborough was the birthplace of inside forward George Gresham. He joined the club from his local team Gainsborough Trinity in 1895. George played a prominent part in the club's early existence as Thames Ironworks. He gained medals for their London League championship in 1898 and the Southern League championship the following season. He ended his career with a total of 110 first-team appearances, scoring some 48 goals.

TUESDAY 19TH JUNE 2001

Hammers' legend and former England international Trevor Brooking was appointed to the club's board of directors as a non-executive director. His newly-formed role was to provide a link between the training ground and the boardroom, as well as adding his playing and coaching experience to help aid the manager and coaching staff on a day-to-day basis.

TUESDAY 20TH JUNE 1911

The birthplace of wing-half Joe Cockroft was Barnsley. Joe came to West Ham at the end of the 1932-33 season. He then went on to be ever-present in four consecutive seasons. In all, he totalled 263 league and cup appearances, scoring three goals. He also gained a winner's medal when the Hammers won the Football League War Cup in 1940. He later played for both Sheffield United and Sheffield Wednesday.

WEDNESDAY 20TH JUNE 1962

The Hammers were in Ghana playing a friendly tour game with Ashanti Kotoko. West Ham won the game 3-0 with ease when Johnny Dick scored twice and Ronnie Boyce added the other.

SUNDAY 20TH JUNE 1965

West Ham played TSV Munich in their second match in the American Soccer League. West Ham had beaten the German side a few months earlier in the final of the European Cup Winners' Cup – and repeated the trick on US soil. They took a third-minute lead through Martin Peters but Munich equalised after ten minutes. West Ham then missed a penalty but gained the winning goal when Alan Sealey headed home nine minutes from time.

TUESDAY 21ST JUNE 1949

England international forward Stuart Pearson was born in Hull. He started his career with Hull City in 1969 and, after 150 games for the east Yorkshire side, he joined Manchester United in 1974 where, in his first season, he won a Second Division Championship medal. He had an excellent time with United, playing in 179 games which included two Wembley FA Cup Finals. Pearson arrived at Upton Park in August 1979 and, a year later, was a member of the Hammers' team that won the 1980 FA Cup Final. He appeared in 50 matches for West Ham, scoring ten goals, and was later assistant manager at both Bradford City and West Bromwich Albion.

SATURDAY 22ND JUNE 2002

After making 27 appearances in a Hammers shirt, the Cameroon captain Rigobert Song joined the German side Cologne. Before joining West Ham he had played in Italy for Salernitana before arriving in England to play for Liverpool where he featured in 38 games for the Reds before switching to West Ham.

SUNDAY 23RD JUNE 1963

The Hammers were in New York for a group match against the French side Valenciennes in the American Soccer League. The star of the match was Geoff Hurst who netted a hat-trick in the 3-1 win.

SUNDAY 24TH JUNE 1962

The final game of the African tour brought West Ham to Ghana to play against Real Republicans. Having won their five previous tour games, this one proved to be harder as the teams drew 1-1 with Malcolm Musgrove netting the Hammers' goal.

MONDAY 25th JUNE 2001

West Ham appointed Ludek Miklosko as their new goalkeeping coach. Ludo had vast experience, having competed 365 times for West Ham and played 65 games for Queens Park Rangers. He had also been capped 44 times by Czechoslovakia.

SUNDAY 26th JUNE 1955

Goalkeeper Mervyn Day was born in Chelmsford, Essex. He made his Hammers debut as an 18-year-old in August 1973 against Ipswich Town. He played 231 games for West Ham and won the 1975 FA Cup and was a runner-up a year later in the European Cup Winners' Cup. He left in 1979 to sign for Orient where he became club captain. Following on from that, there were spells at Aston Villa and Leeds United. After playing in some 700 games he became coach and then manager at Carlisle United. He was assistant manager under Alan Curbishley at Charlton Athletic and later took the same role at West Ham.

WEDNESDAY 26th JUNE 1963

The final game in the American Soccer League paired West Ham with Recife, from Brazil. After Johnny Byrne scored in the 10th minute the Brazilians handed out some rough treatment to the Hammers. They equalised but the game finished 1-1 with West Ham being declared League Winners. This qualified them to meet the other group winners Gornik in two play-off games.

WEDNESDAY 26th JUNE 2002

West Ham signed French Under-18 international striker Youssef Sofiane on a free transfer from Auxerre. He was considered an exciting prospect but the youngster was not able to compete with the rigours of the English game. Sofiane was loaned out to Notts County for a spell but after only two games for West Ham, he returned to France in 2004.

THURSDAY 27th JUNE 2002

After spending six years at Manchester United, Dutch goalkeeper Raimond Van der Gouw joined West Ham on a free transfer. He spent the entire 2002-03 season playing reserve team football and was the first-team substitute goalkeeper. At the end of the season he was one of many players released as the Hammers were relegated.

MONDAY 28TH JUNE 1982

In the World Cup Finals in Spain, West Ham François Van Der Elst came on for Belgium as a second-half substitute in their 3-0 defeat against Poland in Barcelona.

WEDNESDAY 28TH JUNE 2000

American goalkeeper Ian Feuer joined Wimbledon on a free transfer. He had two spells at Upton Park, firstly in 1994 after which he played for Peterborough, Luton Town and Cardiff City. He then joined West Ham again in 2000 where he played in three Premiership games. After going to Wimbledon he was loaned out to Derby County for a spell before returning to the United States.

WEDNESDAY 29TH JUNE 1966

Bobby Moore was captain of the England team that beat Norway 6-1 in Oslo in an international friendly match.

FRIDAY 30TH JUNE 2000

The club paid nearly £2million for the impressive collection of trophies and medals won by former skipper Bobby Moore. The impressive array of memorabilia took pride of place in the club's museum following the purchase from his first wife, Tina.

WEST HAM UNITED
On This Day

JULY

THURSDAY 1st JULY 1965

In their third game in the American International League, West Ham were 2-0 down after just 18 minutes against Brazilian side Portugesa – but fought back with goals from Brian Dear and Tony Scott. Just on half-time, the Brazilians went ahead again and after the interval scored a fourth. Ronnie Boyce kept West Ham in the game with a goal in the 70th minute but Portugesa scored two further goals to win the match 6-3.

FRIDAY 2nd JULY 1965

Popular Hammers full-back Tim Breacker first entered the world in Bicester, Oxfordshire. He joined from Luton Town as Billy Bonds' first signing in October 1990. After making 208 league appearances for the Hatters he now settled for a career at Upton Park. He gave the club ten years' good service, playing in a total of 289 league and cup matches. He left in 1999 to join Queens Park Rangers where he played a further 47 games in three seasons.

SUNDAY 3rd JULY 1966

Ahead of the 1966 World Cup Finals, England played a warm up friendly with Denmark in Copenhagen which resulted in a 2-0 victory. Bobby Moore skippered the side, while Geoff Hurst played up front.

SUNDAY 4th JULY 1965

Games were coming thick and fast in the 1965 American Soccer League tournament. On this day, the Hammers faced the New Yorkers, in New York – but went down 3-1, the goal was scored by Ron Boyce.

THURSDAY 5th JULY 1900

After Thames Ironworks had been wound up the club was reformed on this day under the new name of West Ham United FC. In their first season in the Southern League they finished sixth of fifteen clubs.

MONDAY 5th JULY 1982

Trevor Brooking won his 47th and final England cap in a World Cup phase two group game in Madrid. England drew 0-0 with hosts Spain, but remarkably, despite being undefeated and only conceding once in five games – which included games against France, Germany and Spain – Ron Greenwood's men failed to qualify for the semi-finals!

WEDNESDAY 5TH JULY 2000

In a double swoop the Hammers signed Croatian international Davor Suker on a free transfer and Nigel Winterburn for £250,000 – both joined from Arsenal. At his peak Suker was one of the best strikers in the world and had played for top sides Dynamo Zagreb, Seville and Real Madrid. He was past his best at Upton Park and only managed three goals in thirteen appearances. He was transferred to TSV Munich in 2000. Experienced full-back Winterburn began his career as an apprentice at Birmingham City before joining Wimbledon in 1983, where he made 182 appearances before he signed for Arsenal in 1987. With the Gunners he had an amazing career, winning nearly all the top club honours and playing in a total of 590 games. After coming to West Ham he gave them good service, making 94 appearances in two seasons before retiring and moving into coaching with Blackburn Rovers, under the management of fellow former Hammer Paul Ince in the summer of 2008.

MONDAY 6TH JULY 1981

Preston was the birthplace of midfielder Adam Nowland. He started his career at Blackpool in 1999 and, after three seasons, he had played in 79 games before he joined Wimbledon. With the Dons he made 51 appearances and then came to West Ham in January 2004. He left in November 2004 to join Nottingham Forest.

SATURDAY 7TH JULY 2007

The club issue a statement regarding the impending purchase of Craig Bellamy from Liverpool. It reads: 'After a fee of £7.5million was agreed between the two clubs, we can confirm that the Welsh international captain has successfully passed a medical. However, the deal has been delayed due to a private issue between the player and Liverpool, which must be resolved before any transfer can be completed.'

THURSDAY 8TH JULY 1965

It's the Hammers' fifth game in the American Soccer League against the Italian team Varese. The temperature is a sweltering 85 degrees, but with Johnny Byrne pulling the strings, West Ham take a 2-1 lead with goals from Eddie Bovington and Ken Brown. However, the Italians fight back for a 2-2 draw.

SUNDAY 8th JULY 2001

A team of Hammers veterans played in the Southern Masters five-a-side tournament at the London Arena. They beat Chelsea and Charlton to qualify for the final against Arsenal – and in an exciting finale, the Hammers won 5-4 to lift the cup. The scorers in the final were Steve Whitton, Mark Bowen, Paul Goddard and George Parris (two).

TUESDAY 9th JULY 1968

Future West Ham gladiator Paolo Di Canio is born in Rome. One of the finest players to have ever represented the club, he started out with lowly Terrana in 1996, before going on to play for three of the leading clubs in Italy. He turned out for Lazio, Juventus and AC Milan before moving to Scotland to sign for Celtic in 1996. After 32 games for the Glasgow giants, he moved south to England, joining Sheffield Wednesday. He only played 48 games for the Owls before he had to serve an 11-match ban after pushing over referee Paul Alcock. In January 1999, manager Harry Redknapp paid £1.7million for his services and he quickly became a Hammers legend. Displaying a huge array of talent, he scored 49 goals in his 130 appearances while at Upton Park. After the Hammers were relegated in 2003, he joined Charlton for a spell and later returned to Italy to join his former club Lazio.

MONDAY 10th JULY 2000

Nigerian striker Manny Omoyinmi joined Oxford United on a free transfer. In his five seasons at Upton Park he only played in 12 games, but many will remember him for a smash-and-grab two-goal raid, to rescue a point after coming on as a sub against Crystal Palace in 1998. However, he will also be remembered for his substitute appearance in the League Cup quarter-final tie against Aston Villa in 1999 – which the Hammers won 5-4 on penalties. However, Omoyinmi had already appeared for Gillingham in an earlier round, while on loan there, which meant he was ineligible to play for West Ham. The club were ordered to replay the game, which they lost. Omoyinmi's time at the club ended soon after.

MONDAY 11th JULY 1966

In the opening game in the World Cup Finals, hosts England drew 0-0 with Uruguay at Wembley. Wearing number six for the Three Lions was Bobby Moore, the captain.

TUESDAY 12TH JULY 1949

Midfielder Jimmy Lindsay was born in Hamilton, Scotland. He was signed in 1966 where he had been spotted playing in Scottish junior football. He spent three seasons with the Hammers but did not gain a regular place in the side. After 45 appearances (three goals), he was transferred to Watford in 1971. He later played for Colchester United, Hereford United and Shrewsbury Town.

TUESDAY 13TH JULY 1965

The final game in the American Soccer League ended with a disappointing 2-0 defeat to the Brazilian team Portugesa. Johnny Byrne cracked his ankle bone in this match to add to the woes. The tournament had been a poor one for the Hammers, with high temperatures and lack of atmosphere at the grounds not helping much.

FRIDAY 13TH JULY 2001

Former striker and fans' favourite Paul Goddard was installed as the assistant manager to Glenn Roeder. He had been a former team-mate to Roeder at both Newcastle United and Queens Park Rangers. Goddard left Upton Park in 2003 following the arrival of Alan Pardew as manager.

TUESDAY 13TH JULY 2004

Having lost the play-off final just over six weeks previously, the Hammers kicked off their pre-season tour of Sweden with an easy 5-0 win against Umea FC. Striker Bobby Zamora was on fine form, grabbing a hat-trick, while the other goals coming from Marlon Harewood and Youssef Sofiane.

TUESDAY 14TH JULY 1903

Wing-half Jimmy Collins was born in Brentford and first played in amateur football with Chelmsford, Clapton and Leyton. He joined West Ham in 1923 and after establishing himself in the side became a model of consistency. He stayed at the Hammers for 13 seasons making a total of 336 appearances and scoring three goals. Collins retired from football in 1936 and went into the horticultural trade, but maintained his links with West Ham, becoming a season ticket holder at Upton Park right up until he died in 1977.

TUESDAY 15TH JULY 2003

A pre-season friendly against AFC Bournemouth at Dean Court saw the Hammers romp to an easy 4-0 victory. Don Hutchison scored twice with further goals coming from Joe Cole, who captained the side, and Trevor Sinclair. It was Sinclair's last goal for the club before he departed to Manchester City.

THURSDAY 15TH JULY 2004

West Ham continued their tour of Sweden with a 3-1 win over Sundsvall. After getting a hat-trick in the first game of the tour Bobby Zamora took his tally to five, with two more. The other goal was scored by Marlon Harewood.

SATURDAY 16TH JULY 1966

England's second group game in the 1966 World Cup Finals, with Mexico the opponents at Wembley Stadium. Martin Peters came into the team for the 2-0 victory over the South Americans, and it was he who started both moves that led to both goals. Typically, Bobby Moore had the armband.

SATURDAY 17TH JULY 1999

West Ham entered the Intertoto Cup for the first time. Their first-leg game was at Upton Park where they welcomed the Finnish side Jokerit, and a goal from Paul Kitson in the 18th minute saw the Hammers win 1-0 before an attendance of 11,908.

TUESDAY 17TH JULY 2001

New manager Glenn Roeder paid Aston Villa £3.5m for then England goalkeeper David James. The stopper had started his career with Watford in 1988. After 98 league and cup appearances he moved to Liverpool in 1992 to become a fixture in the Reds' side. He was soon capped by England but after 255 league and cup games for Liverpool, he was on his travels again to join Aston Villa in 1999. He spent two seasons with the Villa before moving to West Ham. At Upton Park he made 96 appearances in two seasons but, as the Hammers were relegated in 2003, he moved on to Manchester City, before linking up with former Hammers manager Harry Redknapp at Portsmouth in 2006.

TUESDAY 18TH JULY 1899

Future Hammers right-back Percy Thorpe was born in Nottingham. Before joining West Ham he had turned out for Blackpool, Reading and Sheffield Wednesday – making a total of 288 Football League appearances with the three clubs. He came to the Hammers in 1933 but only played in the first three games of the season before leaving to join Accrington Stanley.

FRIDAY 19TH JULY 2002

It was a disappointing start to the pre-season warm-up campaign, as the Hammers went down 3-1 to Leyton Orient at Brisbane Road in their first friendly. A crowd of around 4,500 saw Jermain Defoe score the only West Ham goal.

MONDAY 19TH JULY 2004

West Ham completed a hat-trick of wins on their tour of Sweden with a 3-1 victory over First Division side Friska Viljor. Don Hutchison opened the scoring and further goals came from Nigel Reo-Coker and Hayden Mullins.

WEDNESDAY 20TH JULY 1966

Bobby Moore and Martin Peters play prominent roles as England beat France 2-0 at Wembley in a World Cup Finals Group game.

TUESDAY 21ST JULY 1998

A pre-season friendly at nearby neighbours Dagenham & Redbridge results in an easy 3-1 victory for the Hammers, with goals coming from Ian Pearce, Frank Lampard and Lee Hodges.

TUESDAY 22ND JULY 2003

On a trip to Sweden, West Ham came from behind twice to beat Atvidabergs 5-2. Joe Cole and Jermain Defoe scored two each with a further goal from Frenchman Youssef Sofiane. Back in England, on the same day, pacy winger Trevor Sinclair left the club to sign for Manchester City in a transfer deal worth £2.5m. During the five seasons he spent at Upton Park Sinclair had gained 11 England caps under Sven-Göran Eriksson and made a total of 195 league and cup appearances for the Hammers.

TREVOR SINCLAIR

SATURDAY 23RD JULY 1966

The World Cup quarter-final paired England with Argentina at Wembley. A crowd of 90,584 saw England triumph with a narrow 1-0 win. Three Hammers feature in the England team, namely Bobby Moore, Geoff Hurst and Martin Peters. And it's a West Ham connection which creates the England goal: scored by Hurst following a cross from Peters.

WEDNESDAY 23RD JULY 1980

A 6,000 crowd at the Priestfield Stadium sees David Cross's goal give West Ham a 1-0 interval lead in a pre-season friendly with Gillingham. However, the Kent club equalised in the second half and the game ended all square at 1-1.

SATURDAY 24TH JULY 1999

The return leg in the Intertoto Cup saw the Hammers travel to Finland to play Jokerit, already leading 1-0 from the first-leg at Upton Park. The Finns scored first in the 33rd minute to level the scores on aggregate but a second-half goal from Frank Lampard put West Ham through to the next round.

THURSDAY 24TH JULY 2003

The Hammers travelled to Norrtälje – a small town just outside the Swedish capital Stockholm. There they played the Swedish Champions Djurgardens in a pre-season friendly and held the Champions League side to a 0-0 draw.

SATURDAY 24TH JULY 2004

A pre-season friendly against Peterborough United at London Road ended in a 1-1 draw. New signing Teddy Sheringham – the former England striker joined West Ham from Portsmouth on a free transfer – made his West Ham debut but it was midfielder Christian Dailly who scored the Hammers' goal.

THURSDAY 25TH JULY 1974

The first game of the Hammers' tour of Norway was a fixture with First Division Champions Viking played in Stavanger – but it was tough going and the Norwegians' team were the better side, winning 2-0.

FRIDAY 25TH JULY 1980

FA Cup holders West Ham travelled to Layer Road to face Essex club Colchester United in a pre-season friendly. Centre-forward David Cross scores a late goal in a 1-1 draw.

FRIDAY 26TH JULY 2002

There was a 4,309 crowd at Layer Road to see the 1-1 friendly draw with Colchester United in a friendly. Jermain Defoe got the goal.

SATURDAY 27TH JULY 1996

West Ham prepare for a tour of the West Country with a friendly en route at Reading. Ex-players Jimmy Quinn and Trevor Morley were in the Royals' side which the Hammers beat 2-1 in front of 5,796 fans at Reading's old Elm Park Ground, courtesy of goals scored by Robbie Slater and Michael Hughes.

SATURDAY 28TH JULY 1969

FC Cologne provided formidable opposition in the first game of West Ham's tour of Germany. The Germans were too strong and ran out 4-1 winners before a crowd of around 15,000. West Ham's lone scorer was Johnny Sissons.

MONDAY 28TH JULY 1980

A friendly at The Valley saw West Ham beat Charlton Athletic 4-0. Geoff Pike scored twice and there was one apiece for Stuart Pearson and Bobby Barnes to please the Hammers' following in the paltry crowd of just 2,800.

MONDAY 29TH JULY 1974

On tour in Norway the Hammers had an easy 5-0 victory against Second Division outfit Start. Man of the match was Clyde Best, he hit a hat-trick. Bobby Gould and John McDowell were also on the scoresheet.

THURSDAY 29TH JULY 1976

In the opening fixture of a tour of Scandinavia – against Swedish Third Division side Sandakerns – the Hammers won 2-1 with goals from John McDowell and Alan Taylor. Making his Hammers debut at centre-half was new signing Bill Green.

SATURDAY 30TH JULY 1966

The greatest day in English football – and also a very proud day in the history of West Ham United, as three Hammers feature in England's World Cup winning team. Sir Alf Ramsey's team beat West Germany 4-2 at Wembley to win the final, with Geoff Hurst scoring a magnificent hat-trick, Martin Peters getting England's other goal, and Bobby Moore collecting the gold Jules Rimet Trophy from the Queen on an unforgettable afternoon at Wembley.

SUNDAY 30TH JULY 1972

Swedes Halmstad were the opponents on a tour of Sweden, in an end-to-end game West Ham won 5-3. Winger Dudley Tyler scored twice with Clyde Best, Ade Coker and Trevor Brooking also getting goals.

MONDAY 30TH JULY 1979

David Cross was amongst the goals again, this time down on the south coast as the Hammers met Portsmouth in a pre-season friendly. He scored twice in the first half and although Pompey pulled a goal back in the second half it was West Ham who held on to win 2-1, with 6,100 watching on.

WEDNESDAY 31ST JULY 1963

As West Ham had won their group in the American Soccer League they met Gornik from Poland, the other group winners, in New York. The first-leg of the final ended 1-1. Johnny Byrne gave West Ham the lead on 21 minutes but the Poles equalised in the second half.

WEDNESDAY 31ST JULY 1968

A crowd of approximately 5,000 were at Cloppenburg in Germany to watch West Ham play a local amateur combination team. The Hammers ran out easy winners, by an 8-1 margin, with two goals each for Trevor Brooking, Brian Dear and John Sissons, and one each for England stars Geoff Hurst and Martin Peters.

THURSDAY 31ST JULY 1975

FA Cup holders West Ham played their second match on tour in Norway against Lillestrom, and won comfortably 4-1. Graham Paddon scores twice, and Pat Holland and Billy Jennings notch one apiece.

WEST HAM UNITED
On This Day

AUGUST

SATURDAY 1st AUGUST 1970

There were 13,986 spectators at Fratton Park to see Portsmouth play West Ham in a pre-season friendly. First-half goals from Geoff Hurst and Trevor Brooking gave the Hammers a 2-0 win. Israeli captain Mordechai Spiegler played his first game for the club.

TUESDAY 1st AUGUST 1972

The Hammers were on a pre-season tour of Sweden where they met the Belgian side Standard Liège in an exhibition match. Billy Bonds opened the scoring but the Belgians equalised from a penalty and the score finished at 1-1.

TUESDAY 2nd AUGUST 1977

The first match of the tour of Scandinavia took place against SK Brann, winners of the Norwegian Cup. Alan Curbishley scored twice and another goal came from John Radford during a 3-2 victory.

SATURDAY 2nd AUGUST 1980

The Hammers travelled to Scotland where they met Dundee United in the first match of their Scottish tour. An attendance of 5,671 saw the Hammers win 1-0 courtesy of a goal from David Cross.

SUNDAY 2nd AUGUST 1981

West Ham entered a four-team tournament in Aberdeen where they met Manchester United. A single goal from David Cross settled the game in the Hammers' favour.

SATURDAY 3rd AUGUST 1974

A Texaco Cup match with local neighbours Orient at Upton Park attracted a crowd of 16,338. The Hammers won the tie 1-0 thanks to a 23rd-minute goal from Billy Bonds.

FRIDAY 3rd AUGUST 1979

West Ham participated in the annual Tennant Caledonian Cup Tournament played at Ibrox Stadium, Glasgow. The Hammers played the host club Glasgow Rangers before a crowd of around 10,000. The Scottish team won 3-2 – Billy Jennings and David Cross got the goals for West Ham.

SUNDAY 4TH AUGUST 1963

The day of the second-leg of the American Soccer League Final with Poles Gornik. Level at 1-1 after the first-leg, Geoff Hurst scored just before half-time. In the second half Gornik had two goals disallowed, causing a pitch invasion and the referee was attacked. It took half an hour for order to be restored; thankfully the game carried on without further incident and the Hammers held on to be crowned champions, and qualified to meet Dukla Prague, the holders, in the Challenge Cup Final.

WEDNESDAY 4TH AUGUST 1999

West Ham travelled to Holland to play Heerenveen in the second-leg of the Intertoto Cup. Leading 1-0 from the first-leg, a goal from Paulo Wanchope gave them another 1-0 victory and a place in the final.

SATURDAY 5TH AUGUST 1972

The final game of the Swedish tour saw the Hammers play First Division Oester. The game was goalless at half-time, but Frank Lampard and Pop Robson were on the scoresheet in the second half for a 2-0 victory.

TUESDAY 5TH AUGUST 1975

While touring in Norway, West Ham played against Second Division Alesund. An easy 5-1 win for the Hammers. Bobby Gould scored two and Graham Paddon, Alan Taylor and Tommy Taylor get a goal each.

SATURDAY 5TH AUGUST 1978

A pre-season friendly at Swindon Town saw the Hammers win 3-2 with goals from Alan Devonshire, Trevor Brooking and Pop Robson. Goalkeeper Bobby Ferguson was injured in the first half and without a substitute goalkeeper Trevor Brooking took over between the sticks.

FRIDAY 6TH AUGUST 1971

Full-back Scott Minto was born at Heswall, Cheshire. He began his career at Charlton Athletic in 1989, playing in 205 league games before being transferred to Chelsea in May 1994. With the Blues he made 72 league appearances before switching to Benfica in 1997, where he played 31 games. He came to West Ham for a fee of £1 million in January 1999. In three seasons at Upton Park he made a total of 62 appearances before he moved to Rotherham United, where he finished his playing career.

FRIDAY 6TH AUGUST 1982

Playing in a four-team tournament in Belgium the Hammers' first match was against Anderlecht – who had beaten West Ham six years earlier in the 1976 Cup Winners Cup Final. On this occasion they got their revenge as Geoff Pike netted the only goal of the game in the 68th minute.

SATURDAY 7TH AUGUST 1965

West Ham embarked on a short tour of Germany where they met Eintracht Frankfurt. Brian Dear had an early goal disallowed but West Ham eventually took the lead through a header from Martin Peters. On the hour the Germans equalised – but with seven minutes remaining Alan Sealey scored to give the Hammers a 2-1 win.

FRIDAY 7TH AUGUST 1970

A crowd of 13,321 was at Brisbane Road to see the friendly with the Orient. A converted penalty gave the home side the lead in the second half – but West Ham equalised five minutes from time with a goal from Peter Eustace.

WEDNESDAY 7TH AUGUST 1974

A Texaco Cup match at Upton Park against Luton Town saw the Hatters take a 2-0 lead during the second half – and although Billy Bonds scored from a penalty in the 73rd minute, it was Luton who ran out 2-1 winners.

TUESDAY 8TH AUGUST 1950

Sedgeley, in the West Midlands, was the birthplace of giant goalkeeper Phil Parkes. He began his career with his local club Walsall in 1969 and, after 52 games for them, he came to London to play for Queens Park Rangers in 1970. He spent nine seasons at Loftus Road, playing in a total of 406 games and, while there, he gained an England cap against Portugal in 1974. In February 1979, West Ham paid £565,000 for his services – a then world record fee for a goalkeeper. With the Hammers he had a brilliant career, wining an FA Cup Winners' medal in 1980 and, a year later, he was in the Second Division Championship-winning side. He spent 12 seasons with West Ham – playing in a total of 436 games – before leaving in 1990 to join Ipswich Town as a goalkeeping coach.

SUNDAY 8TH AUGUST 1982

The final of the four-team tournament in Belgium was between West Ham and Hadjuk Split. The game ended goalless so was decided on penalties. The best of five kicks apiece ended 4-4 – but sudden death saw West Ham miss. Hadjuk Split then scored to win the trophy.

MONDAY 9TH AUGUST 1971

A trip to Scotland to play a friendly with Dunfermline Athletic at East End Park saw the Scottish team take the lead on 30 minutes – but Geoff Hurst equalised a minute from half-time. In the second half it was Hurst again who scored to give West Ham the lead, and he completed his hat-trick in the 70th minute, to give the Hammers a 3-1 win.

SATURDAY 9TH AUGUST 1975

There were 59,000 at Wembley Stadium for the Charity Shield game between FA Cup holders West Ham and Football League Champions Derby County. On a swelteringly hot day it was the Rams who were on top throughout, winning the game 2-0.

THURSDAY 9TH AUGUST 1979

West Ham were in Scotland to play a friendly against the then Highland League side Ross County. It was a one-sided affair, with the Hammers crushing their amateur opponents 8-1. Scoring two each were David Cross and Pat Holland, while further strikes came from Paul Brush, Billy Jennings, Dale Banton and Billy Lansdowne.

WEDNESDAY 10TH AUGUST 1966

On a continental tour, West Ham visited Switzerland to play Lausanne. The Hammers raced into a 2-0 lead in the first half; both goals came from Johnny Byrne. In a game of two halves, it was the Swiss team who fought back to claim two goals to ensure the match finished level at 2-2.

THURSDAY 10TH AUGUST 1978

A trip to Norway for West Ham, where they played Allesund and renewed acquaintances with ex-Hammer Bobby Gould who was the Norwegians' coach. It was an easy victory for the Hammers. Pop Robson and Alan Taylor netted one each before half-time and David Cross added two more for a 4-0 success.

SATURDAY 11TH AUGUST 1973

The Watney Cup paired Bristol Rovers with West Ham at Eastville. On a very hot day in Bristol a close encounter between the two teams ended 1-1. The hosts had taken the lead but Ted MacDougall levelled the scores after 38 minutes. Rovers won a penalty shoot-out 6-5.

THURSDAY 11TH AUGUST 1977

To warm up for the new season, the Hammers entered a four-team tournament in Spain where their first game was against Real Majorca. West Ham put on a good performance to win 4-0. The goals were scored by Alan Curbishley, Bill Green, John Radford and Alan Taylor.

WEDNESDAY 11TH AUGUST 1999

The first-leg of the Intertoto Cup Final was played at Upton Park against the French team Metz. It was a night of disappointment for the 25,372 spectators as Frank Lampard missed a penalty and Metz went into the second-leg with a 1-0 lead.

THURSDAY 12TH AUGUST 1976

The Hammers were in Spain for the Prince Felipe Tournament. After a draw with Belenenses, they met hosts Real Santander. The score was 2-2 – Graham Paddon got both – and there were 12 minutes left, when Billy Jennings got injured. The only available sub was keeper Bobby Ferguson, who came off the bench to score the winner in the last minute!

SATURDAY 12TH AUGUST 2006

West Ham played a home friendly with the Greek side Olympiakos. A crowd of around 14,000 – braving a cold and wet day – were cheered by a terrific solo goal from Marlon Harewood after 24 minutes. The Greeks scored an equaliser after the break and the game ended 1-1.

SATURDAY 13TH AUGUST 1966

Continuing their Euro tour West Ham played Germans Karlsruhe before a huge crowd of 27,000. A fortnight after helping England beat West Germany in the World Cup Final, Bobby Moore, Geoff Hurst and Martin Peters were an attraction. Just as the 90 minutes had ended at Wembley, this game was 2-2 with the German equaliser coming in the last minute... And of course, the scorers were Peters and Hurst!

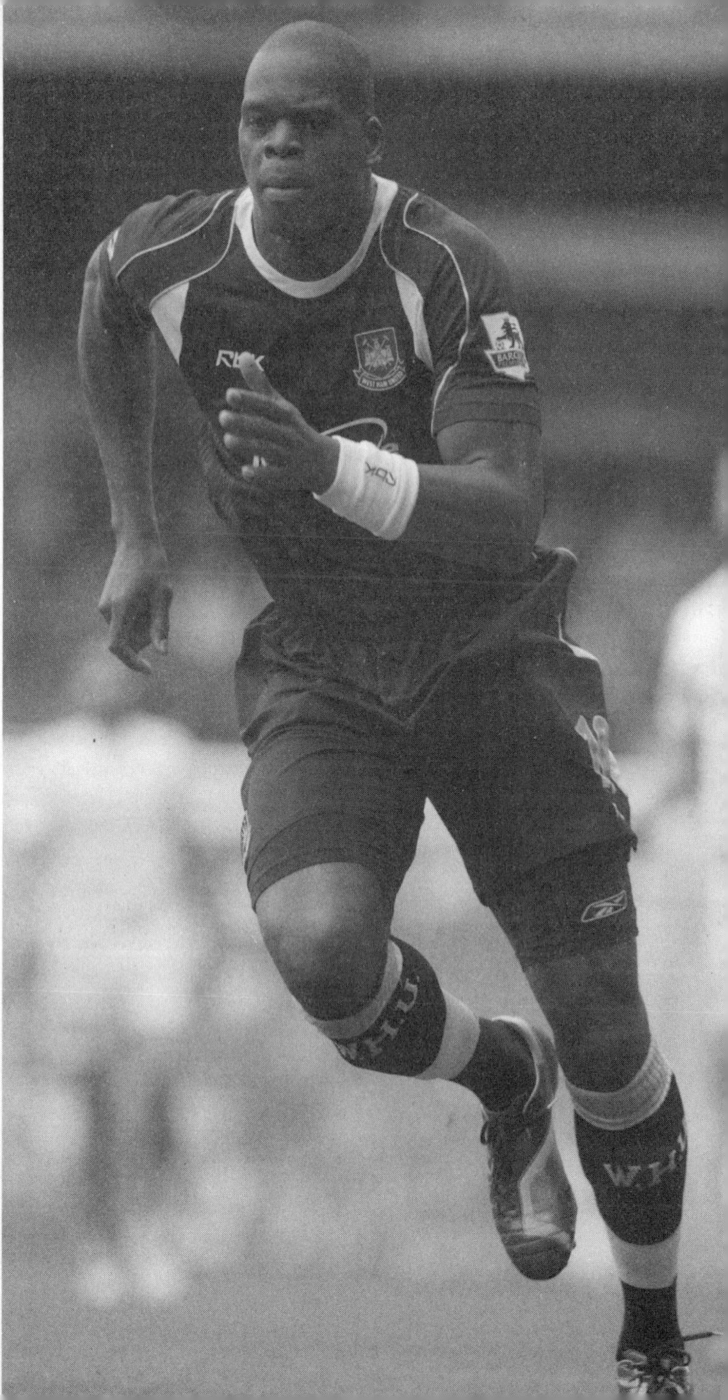

MARLON HAREWOOD IN ACTION AGAINST OLYMPIAKOS

SATURDAY 13TH AUGUST 1977

The Hammers were playing the Spanish team Betis in the final of a four-team tournament in Majorca. The game ended 0-0 with the resulting penalty shoot-out won 6-5 by Betis.

WEDNESDAY 14TH AUGUST 1968

A midweek First Division game away at Stoke City's Victoria Ground brought a welcome 2-0 victory for West Ham. It was nil-nil at half-time, but Martin Peters scored from a pass from Johnny Sissons, with Sissons on hand to add the second.

MONDAY 14TH AUGUST 1972

The first home game of the season brought Coventry City to Upton Park. Not the best of games for the 27,498 spectators but a good start nonetheless and the home fans went away happy after a 1-0 victory. The only goal: a header from Clyde Best.

SATURDAY 15TH AUGUST 1964

The 38,858 spectators at Anfield enjoyed a pulsating game as League Champions Liverpool entertained FA Cup holders West Ham in the annual Charity Shield. After the Reds took the lead it was Johnny Byrne who equalised minutes before half-time. In the second half again Liverpool took the lead but, with six minutes remaining, Geoff Hurst netted an equaliser meaning the trophy was shared, and held by each team for six months apiece.

SUNDAY 15TH AUGUST 1982

West Ham were in Holland for a pre-season friendly with Dutch First Division side Den Haag. The game looked to be heading for a draw – it was goalless until the 83rd minute, when Geoff Pike put the Hammers ahead. Then, in a torrential downpour, West Ham scored again a minute from time through François Van Der Elst to finish 2-0 winners.

SATURDAY 15TH AUGUST 1998

The opening league game of the season saw West Ham play at Hillsborough against Sheffield Wednesday. It was an even affair with the two sides cancelling each other out, until new signing Ian Wright popped up in the 84th minute to score the winner on his debut.

SATURDAY 16TH AUGUST 1975

West Ham began the new season as FA Cup holders, kicking off at Stoke City. Wembley hero Alan Taylor scored the first and Bobby Gould added another to put the Hammers firmly in control. Stoke were finally beaten 2-1 – they scored a consolation two minutes from time.

SATURDAY 16TH AUGUST 1981

West Ham opened the season with a home match against Luton Town – which turned out to be a game of three penalties. Ray Stewart scored from the spot to put the Hammers ahead – but the Hatters came back to win 2-1 after they converted two spot-kicks. A defeat on the first home game was disappointing – but it turned out to be the only home defeat of the season!

MONDAY 16TH AUGUST 1999

The first away game of the campaign was at Aston Villa. West Ham were gifted an early own-goal but Villa equalised in the first half. After the interval the Hammers went behind; in injury-time, Trevor Sinclair grabbed the equaliser for a 2-2 draw.

TUESDAY 17TH AUGUST 1982

To celebrate their 75th anniversary, the HJK club from Helsinki invited West Ham to Finland for a friendly match. An attendance of 6,380 saw Alan Devonshire net in the 68th minute – the only goal of the contest.

TUESDAY 17TH AUGUST 2004

Anton Ferdinand won his first England under-21 cap against Ukraine at Middlesbrough. Fellow Hammer Nigel Reo-Coker came on as a sub.

SATURDAY 18TH AUGUST 1956

West Ham kicked off the new season with a bang away to neighbours Fulham with a 4-1 win. On the scoresheet were Billy Dare (two), Mike Grice and Ken Tucker.

SATURDAY 18TH AUGUST 1979

The Hammers opened their Second Division campaign at Wrexham as promotion favourites – but in a disappointing display they lost 1-0. Stuart Pearson – signed from Manchester United – made his debut.

SATURDAY 18th AUGUST 2001

Glenn Roeder was in charge for the first time when West Ham played Liverpool at Anfield. West Ham's record at Anfield going into the game was appalling and on this occasion it didn't get any better. Paolo Di Canio scored from a penalty but two goals from Michael Owen were enough to give the Reds a winning start.

MONDAY 19th AUGUST 1968

The Hammers were unbeaten in their first three league games and going into a home game with Everton they knew another win would put them top of the First Division. Alas, Everton took full advantage of some poor defending to win 4-1. The Hammers' lone goal was scored by Martin Peters.

SATURDAY 19th AUGUST 1972

Striker Pop Robson scored twice as Leicester City were beaten 5-2 at Upton Park. Leicester took the lead after three minutes and played well in the early stages – but eventually the Hammers took control. Dudley Tyler scored his first goal for the club and further strikes came from Ade Coker and Bobby Moore.

SATURDAY 20th AUGUST 1960

The Football League campaign started at Molineux and Wolverhampton Wanderers found themselves a goal down when Johnny Dick scored after seven minutes. However, Wolves – inspired by England's Ronnie Flowers – came back with four goals. A late goal from Phil Woosnam was not enough to help launch a West Ham comeback as the home side won the game 4-2.

SATURDAY 20th AUGUST 1966

All eyes were on the trio of Bobby Moore, Geoff Hurst and Martin Peters as they came onto the Upton Park pitch before the other players to receive a rousing reception from the Hammers' fans for their efforts in helping England to win the World Cup at Wembley earlier that summer. There were 36,126 fans packed inside Upton Park for the First Division London derby with Chelsea. Ronnie Boyce scored for the Hammers but the Blues – with keeper Peter Bonetti in fine form – clinched local bragging rights, winning the game 2-1.

TUESDAY 20TH AUGUST 1985

The first home game of what would turn out to be a very exciting season and the Hammers recorded a 3-1 win over Queens Park Rangers. Scottish striker Frank McAvennie was making his home debut and he celebrated with two goals. Alan Dickens headed the other goal.

MONDAY 21ST AUGUST 1967

After an opening-day defeat the Hammers bounced back with an emphatic 4-2 victory against Burnley at Upton Park. Trailing 1-0 at the interval, West Ham crushed the Clarets with four second half goals from Martin Peters, Geoff Hurst (two), and Harry Redknapp.

FRIDAY 21ST AUGUST 1981

For the third successive season, West Ham played at Southend United in a pre-season friendly. A crowd of 7,186 saw Alvin Martin open the scoring in the first minute, and although the Shrimpers fought back to equalise, David Cross netted the Hammers' winner after 65 minutes.

SATURDAY 21ST AUGUST 1988

A well-deserved testimonial match for the West Ham skipper Alvin Martin and Tottenham Hotspur provided the opposition for a lively contest that the Hammers won 2-0. Tony Gale opened the scoring with a tremendous shot after 33 minutes. Substitute Paul Hilton added to the score. Alvin Martin enjoyed a great career at Upton Park, playing in a total of 586 league and cup games.

MONDAY 22ND AUGUST 1960

The opening home game of the season left most of the 28,959 crowd pleased as West Ham beat Aston Villa 5-2. It was great to watch with seven different scorers. Hitting the net for West Ham were John Bond, Johnny Dick, Dave Dunmore, Malcolm Musgrove and Phil Woosnam.

SATURDAY 22ND AUGUST 1970

For the third successive match West Ham were involved in a London derby. On this day they were at home to Chelsea and preserved an unbeaten record with a 2-2 draw. The Hammers raced into a two-goal lead courtesy of strikes from Bobby Howe and Geoff Hurst, but the Blues hit back with both goals coming from Keith Weller.

SATURDAY 22ND AUGUST 1987

West Ham and Luton Town both picked up their first point of the season as they drew 2-2 at Kenilworth Road. Liam Brady and Ray Stewart – converting a penalty – were the Hammers' goalscorers. In the Luton team were three players who would later sign for West Ham: Les Sealey, Tim Breacker and Mike Newell.

MONDAY 23RD AUGUST 1954

A terrible start to the new campaign continued. After a 5-2 defeat at Swansea on the opening day, West Ham were beaten by the same score by Blackburn Rovers at Ewood Park three days later. A week later, West Ham slumped to a third successive 5-2 defeat, as Blackburn won at Upton Park. Goalkeeper Peter Chiswick never played again for the club.

WEDNESDAY 23RD AUGUST 1961

A thrilling London Derby for those who witnessed Tottenham v West Ham at White Hart Lane on this day. Spurs – who had won the double the previous season – took an early lead but Phil Woosnam equalised just before half-time, before Malcolm Musgrove gave West Ham the lead. Terry Dyson came to the rescue for Spurs with an equalising goal. The 2-2 draw was a fair result and great entertainment for the 50,214 fans.

THURSDAY 24TH AUGUST 1950

Midfielder Graham Paddon was born in Manchester. He served both Norwich City and West Ham well. A great club man, he had two spells at Norwich playing in a total of 340 games scoring 37 goals. He joined West Ham in 1973 and went on to gain an FA Cup winners' medal in 1975 and a year later, was a runner-up in the European Cup Winners' Cup Final. Graham scored 15 goals while with the Hammers and played in a total of 150 senior matches. He later coached at Portsmouth and was assistant boss at Stoke City. He sadly died in November 2007, aged 57.

WEDNESDAY 24TH AUGUST 1999

A great night in France as the Hammers won the Intertoto Cup against Metz – despite trailing 1-0 from the first-leg. Paolo Di Canio made the first goal for Trevor Sinclair then Frank Lampard scored with a volley. The French hosts pulled a goal back but Paulo Wanchope scored the third and the Hammers held on for a 3-2 aggregate victory.

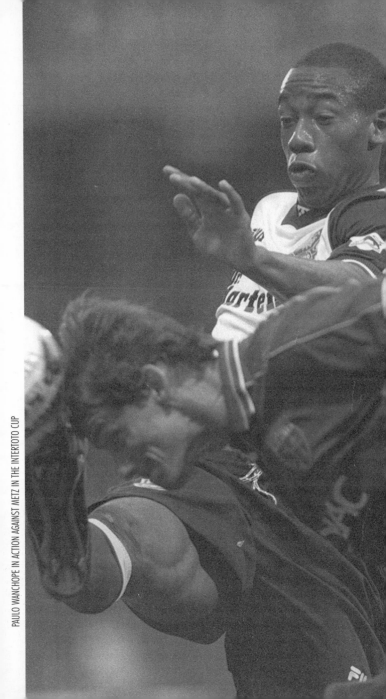

SATURDAY 24TH AUGUST 2002

League Champions Arsenal visited Upton Park for the opening home game of the season. West Ham scored first through Joe Cole and added a second when Fredi Kanoute scored in the second half – but a penalty miss by Kanoute proved a turning point in the game as the Gunners fought back with two late goals to equalise at 2-2.

MONDAY 25TH AUGUST 1958

The gates were closed at Upton Park with thousands locked out (the author of this book being one of them)! Newly-promoted West Ham were playing League Champions Wolverhampton Wanderers. There was a terrific atmosphere inside the ground, as the Hammers turned on the style to win 2-0 with goals from Johnny Dick and John Smith.

SATURDAY 25TH AUGUST 1962

A disaster day at Upton Park as rivals Tottenham crushed West Ham 6-1. It started badly, as John Lyall scored an own-goal and the Hammers were not able to control the threat of Jimmy Greaves, who plundered a brace. A lone goal from Phil Woosnam was scant consolation for the disgruntled home faithful.

SATURDAY 26TH AUGUST 1939

The season began with a Second Division home fixture with Plymouth Argyle. Cliff Hubbard scored twice and a further goal from Jackie Wood ensured a 3-1 victory. A week later the war broke out and the Football League was cancelled with this fixture being deleted from the records.

MONDAY 26TH AUGUST 1968

Burnley were outclassed at Upton Park as the Hammers went to the top of the league with a 5-0 win. The Clarets were overwhelmed in the first half as West Ham built up a four-goal lead with goals from Geoff Hurst (two), Trevor Brooking and Martin Peters.

TUESDAY 26TH AUGUST 1980

Third Division Burnley were brushed aside in this first-leg tie in the League Cup at Turf Moor. New signing Paul Goddard scored his first goal for the club with a volley after 14 minutes and David Cross added a second in the 2-0 win.

MONDAY 27TH AUGUST 1923

After winning promotion West Ham played Arsenal in their first home game in Division One. An attendance of 25,000 at the afternoon game saw the Hammers win 1-0 with a goal from Bert Fletcher.

SATURDAY 27TH AUGUST 1949

A Second Division home game with Barnsley attracted a crowd of 27,541 to Upton Park. The Yorkshiremen were beaten 2-1 with goals from Ken Bainbridge and Danny McGowan. The goal scored by Bainbridge was the fastest-ever goal scored on the ground, timed at just nine seconds.

SATURDAY 28TH AUGUST 1999

The Hammers – still unbeaten – moved into fourth place in the Premiership table after a 3-0 victory at Bradford City. Paolo Di Canio and Trevor Sinclair were first-half scorers while Paulo Wanchope added another just after the break.

SATURDAY 28TH AUGUST 2004

In a Championship match, midfielder Adam Nowland scored his first goal for the club in the 1-0 win against Burnley at Upton Park. In the final minute of the game, young full-back Chris Cohen was sent off after a rash tackle.

SATURDAY 29TH AUGUST 1942

The opening game of the wartime season produced a goal glut for the 8,000 or so who assembled at Fratton Park to see Portsmouth take on the Hammers. It was a nine-goal thriller with West Ham coming out on top to win 5-4. Sammy Small scored twice with one each from George Foreman, Len Goulden and Joe Foxall.

TUESDAY 29TH AUGUST 1967

It seems West Ham have often faced Burnley during the month of August. This match between the two clubs was memorable for an eighteen-year-old Trevor Brooking's full debut for the club. The two teams fought out a thrilling 3-3 draw at Turf Moor. The Hammers' goals were scored by the World Cup winning trio of Bobby Moore, Geoff Hurst and Martin Peters.

SATURDAY 29TH AUGUST 1970

Geoff Hurst stunned the majority of the 50,676 fans at Old Trafford by scoring as early as the second minute. However, Manchester United equalised after 15 minutes – but that was it as far as goals were concerned, and the score remained 1-1 to the end. Billy Bonds had a fine game keeping majestic winger George Best quiet.

SATURDAY 30TH AUGUST 1919

A notable day in West Ham's history: they played their first game in the Football League. There were around 20,000 at Upton Park for the visit of Lincoln City. The visitors went ahead with a penalty but the Hammers equalised before the end through Jimmy Moyes.

SATURDAY 30TH AUGUST 1958

Newly-promoted West Ham crushed Aston Villa in a resounding 7-2 win at Upton Park. The 30,506 crowd were delighted as the Hammers took a 6-0 lead. Easing up slightly, they allowed the Villa two goals – but Johnny Dick struck late for the seventh. Three players scored a brace each; namely Vic Keeble, Dick and Malcolm Musgrove. Wing half Billy Lansdowne got the other goal.

SATURDAY 30TH AUGUST 1980

The Hammers were the promotion favourites and brushed aside Notts County with an emphatic 4-0 win at Upton Park. Leading 1-0 at half-time from a David Cross header, West Ham dominated after the interval. Paul Goddard grabbed two and Ray Stewart netted a penalty.

MONDAY 31ST AUGUST 1931

The season's opening home game was a London derby with Chelsea. The Hammers made it two straight wins with Vic Watson, Tony Weldon and Fred Norris getting the goals in a 3-1 victory. A good start to the campaign – but at the end of the season West Ham were relegated.

SATURDAY 31ST AUGUST 1985

Frank McAvennie announced himself to the football world. The home game with Liverpool beamed around the world, and McAvennie revelled in the limelight as he twice gave West Ham the lead – but on each occasion the Reds equalised to draw the game 2-2.

WEST HAM UNITED
On This Day

SEPTEMBER

SATURDAY 1st SEPTEMBER 1900

This date marked the first-ever game played under the club's new name of West Ham United. A crowd of 2,000 was at the Memorial Grounds to see the home game with Gravesend United, and it took just five minutes for the club to get their first-ever goal with Billy Grassam putting West Ham ahead. In a fine team performance, West Ham went on to win 7-0, with Grassam claiming four, James Reid two and one for Fergus Hunt.

MONDAY 1st SEPTEMBER 1930

Liverpool visited Upton Park and found themselves two goals down after just ten minutes. The Hammers were far too good for the Merseyside outfit, thrashing them 7-0. Prolific scorer Vic Watson finished with a personal tally of four. Stan Earle hit two, and Wilf James the other one. The only disappointment was that a rather paltry gate of just 11,682 was present to witness such a fine victory.

SATURDAY 1st SEPTEMBER 1962

A local derby at newly-promoted Leyton Orient drew a First Division crowd of 23,918 to Brisbane Road. It didn't start well for West Ham as they fell behind after six minutes when ex-Hammer Dave Dunmore scored – and things didn't get much better as they eventually lost 2-0.

MONDAY 2nd SEPTEMBER 1946

The Football League had resumed normal service after the war with clubs beginning the new season in the same division they'd ended the 1938/39 season. The first home game brought a visit from Fulham. The Cottagers had been beaten 7-2 at Bury on the opening day and West Ham added to their woes with a 3-2 win. Scottish inside forward Archie Macaulay scored two and Sammy Small netted the other goal.

SATURDAY 2nd SEPTEMBER 1967

League Champions Manchester United were at Upton Park for a First Division fixture. After an uneventful first half – the game was goalless at half-time – the match exploded into life as United scored two goals within a minute in the second half to take control. Martin Peters scored with a header to give the Hammers brief hope, but the Reds killed the game with a third to win 3-1.

WEDNESDAY 2ND SEPTEMBER 1992

West Ham played in the Anglo-Italian Cup for the first time. Initially they were in a group with all English sides and were drawn at home to Bristol Rovers. For goalkeeper Steve Banks it was his only first-team appearance for the club. There was a meagre crowd of just 4,809 present to see the teams draw 2-2, with both Hammers' goals coming from Julian Dicks.

SATURDAY 3RD SEPTEMBER 1910

The opening game of the Southern League season was against the nearby Essex outfit Southend United. In a game of mixed fortunes, the teams drew 3-3 with the Hammers' goalscorers being Herbert Ashton, Fred Blackburn and George Webb.

WEDNESDAY 3RD SEPTEMBER 1975

The first-leg of the Anglo-Italian Cup Winners' Cup Final was played in Florence against Fiorentina. The Italians scored after 19 minutes and kept their lead until the end to win 1-0.

SATURDAY 4TH SEPTEMBER 1965

A thrilling contest at Bramall Lane as Sheffield United scored three first-half goals against the Hammers. Also in the first half, Geoff Hurst had netted once. After the break West Ham fought back to level the scores, as Joe Kirkup scored and Johnny Byrne grabbed the equaliser – but two late goals for the hosts, however, condemned the Hammers to a 5-3 defeat.

TUESDAY 4TH SEPTEMBER 1984

A sparse crowd of just 14,949 was at Upton Park for the game against Coventry City, in which Greg Campbell made his West Ham debut. The Hammers were awarded two penalties which were both converted by Ray Stewart, and Tony Cottee scored to make the game safe. Nine minutes from time Stuart Pearce – who later joined West Ham – scored a consolation goal for the Sky Blues in their 3-1 defeat.

TUESDAY 4TH SEPTEMBER 2001

In the European Championship, England's under-21 side beat Albania 5-0 at Middlesbrough, and scoring one of the five goals for England was West Ham striker Jermain Defoe.

SATURDAY 5th SEPTEMBER 1992

Cousins Clive and Martin Allen were both on the scoresheet for West Ham in this 2-1 home win over Watford.

TUESDAY 5th SEPTEMBER 2000

West Ham made the long trip to Sunderland and returned with a point after drawing 1-1. Croatian international Davor Suker grabbed an equaliser in the 32nd minute – his second goal for the club.

SATURDAY 6th SEPTEMBER 1930

Having beaten Liverpool 7-0 the previous Saturday, West Ham had high hopes as they travelled to Aston Villa. Vic Watson scored for the Hammers but Villa scored six, with four coming from England international Tom Waring.

SATURDAY 6th SEPTEMBER 1941

A crazy goal feast at Stamford Bridge saw the Hammers beat Chelsea 8-4. There were only 6,427 who saw the wartime league match, as George Foreman, who went on to score 28 goals that season, scored a hat-trick. Joining in the goal spree were Ted Fenton, Sam Small, Len Goulden and Joe Foxall (two).

SATURDAY 6th SEPTEMBER 1958

Unbeaten in the First Division, West Ham looked to continue that run when they took on Luton Town at Kenilworth Road. The game started well for the Hammers, with Vic Keeble putting them ahead, a lead which they held until half-time, but the second half was a disaster as West Ham crumbled and Luton won 4-1.

FRIDAY 6th SEPTEMBER 2002

Joe Cole and Trevor Sinclair were in the England under-21 side which drew 1-1 with Yugoslavia at Bolton Wanderers' Reebok Stadium.

MONDAY 7th SEPTEMBER 1964

A visit from Wolverhampton Wanderers saw West Ham play some exhilarating soccer as the men from the Black Country were crushed 5-0. The 26,879 spectators were treated to goals from Geoff Hurst (two), Johnny Byrne, John Sissons and Bobby Moore.

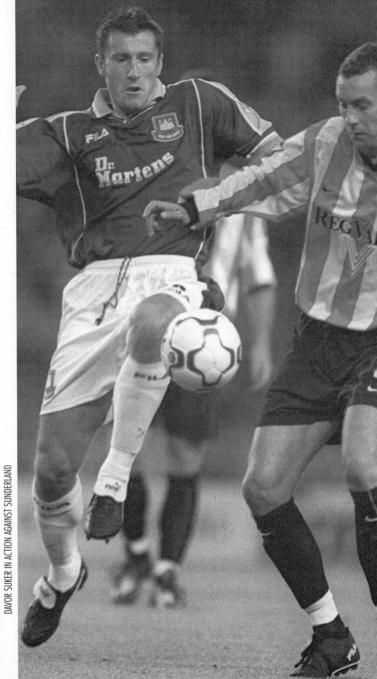

SATURDAY 7TH SEPTEMBER 1985

The start of one of the greatest goalscoring partnerships in West Ham's history! Tony Cottee and Frank McAvennie scored a goal apiece in a 2-2 draw with Sheffield Wednesday at Hillsborough. Between them they scored 46 league goals that season.

MONDAY 8TH SEPTEMBER 1958

A great night for West Ham as they beat Manchester United 3-2 to go top of the league. They were leading 3-0 after an hour thanks to goals from Johnny Dick, John Smith and Malcolm Musgrove. United fought back with two late goals but the Hammers held on to make it a very special night for young debutant Bobby Moore, who was making his first senior appearance for the Hammers.

SATURDAY 8TH SEPTEMBER 1962

The Hammers travelled to Manchester City with only one win to their name, however, they came away with a handsome 6-1 victory. The goals flowed from Tony Scott, Martin Peters, Johnny Byrne, Geoff Hurst and Malcolm Musgrove, who scored twice. City's German keeper Bert Trautmann was sent off for arguing about the fifth goal.

WEDNESDAY 9TH SEPTEMBER 1936

An amazing debut for centre forward Tudor Martin who scored a hat-trick playing against Newcastle United at St James's Park. The feat was somewhat overshadowed by the fact that the Hammers lost 5-3.

SATURDAY 9TH SEPTEMBER 1967

Bobby Moore scored an own-goal to give Sunderland a 1-0 half-time lead in a First Division game at Roker Park. But this was a game of two halves as the Hammers scored three goals in three minutes through Martin Peters, Geoff Hurst and Harry Redknapp. Hurst and Moore – this time at the right end – scored again for a splendid 5-1 win.

WEDNESDAY 9TH SEPTEMBER 1998

A home game to forget! After 27 minutes, West Ham were winning 3-0 against Wimbledon, as Ian Wright scored twice and John Hartson once. But, then came a complete collapse as West Ham allowed the Dons to win 4-3, leaving the home fans in disbelief.

SATURDAY 10TH SEPTEMBER 1983

The Hammers went from despair to delight in a thrilling home league game with Coventry City. The Sky Blues took a two-goal lead and then West Ham missed a penalty. But, inspired by Billy Bonds, there was a terrific come-back as Steve Whitton scored twice and Dave Swindlehurst netted a hat-trick to record a sensational 5-2 win.

WEDNESDAY 10TH SEPTEMBER 1997

Playing in a World Cup qualifier for Northern Ireland were the Hammers trio of Iain Dowie, Steve Lomas and Keith Rowland. They couldn't stop the Irish losing though; they went down 1-0 to Albania.

WEDNESDAY 10TH SEPTEMBER 2003

In Dortmund, Hammer Christian Dailly won his 48th cap for Scotland in their European Championship match against Germany. It was a game which the Scots lost 2-1.

FRIDAY 11TH SEPTEMBER 1964

Born in Ilford on this day was popular full-back George Parris. He signed for the Hammers in July 1981 and played for the reserves for a few seasons before making his first team debut against Liverpool in May 1985. He gave the club sterling service in playing a total of 290 league and cup games, scoring 17 goals. He was transferred to Birmingham City in March 1993 where he went on to play in 42 games. After playing for Brighton & Hove Albion on loan he later joined them on a free transfer in September 1995, recording 56 appearances on the south coast. He retired in 1997 after playing one game for Southend United.

SATURDAY 11TH SEPTEMBER 1982

The home game with Birmingham City marked the 500th league appearance of Frank Lampard. The Hammers celebrated by beating the Blues 5-0. Sandy Clark scored his first goal for the club with the other four coming from Paul Goddard, Ray Stewart, Alvin Martin and François Van Der Elst.

SATURDAY 11TH SEPTEMBER 1999

Watford were at Upton Park for a game in which Stuart Pearce broke his leg. The only goal was scored by Paolo Di Canio from a free-kick.

SATURDAY 12TH SEPTEMBER 1959

West Ham were third in the table and looking for an away win at lowly Bolton Wanderers. The teams were drawing 1-1 at half-time with the Hammers' scorer being Vic Keeble. It was a sorry second half, though, as Bolton piled on four goals to win 5-1.

SATURDAY 12TH SEPTEMBER 1964

A thrilling London derby with rivals Tottenham Hotspur at Upton Park and a game remembered for two brilliant strikers. For Spurs, Jimmy Greaves scored twice – one a penalty. For the Hammers, Johnny Byrne scored a glorious hat-trick in the 3-2 victory – that after missing an early penalty!

WEDNESDAY 13TH SEPTEMBER 1967

Third Division Walsall were at home to the Hammers in a second round League Cup tie. After Peter Brabrook scored two minutes in it was easy for West Ham, who won 5-1. A penalty from Geoff Hurst, two goals from Martin Peters and an own goal completed the scoring.

SATURDAY 13TH SEPTEMBER 1975

West Ham conceded two goals at Leicester City in the first ten minutes and, after an hour, found themselves 3-0 down – but in a remarkable comeback, Billy Bonds, Frank Lampard and Pat Holland, in the last minute, scored to give the Hammers a 3-3 draw.

SATURDAY 13TH SEPTEMBER 1986

A crowd of 16,257 were at Loftus Road for Queens Park Rangers' league game with West Ham. Striker Tony Cottee had just been capped by England and celebrated this with a well taken hat-trick. It was a thrilling game in which Rangers played their part – and were unlucky to lose – as the Hammers ran out only marginal 3-2 winners.

WEDNESDAY 14TH SEPTEMBER 1966

West Ham faced London rivals Tottenham Hotspur in the League Cup – and it was Spurs' first-ever tie in the cup competition. It proved an unhappy debut for the north London side, as they were reduced to ten men when Alan Gilzean was sent off in the second half, and they lost the match 1-0, Geoff Hurst getting the goal.

GEOFF HURST

WEDNESDAY 14TH SEPTEMBER 2006

It was a European night at Upton Park as West Ham welcomed Palermo in a UEFA cup tie. The sell-out crowd of 32,222 looked forward to the debut of top Argentinian signing Javier Mascherano – but it turned out to be a disappointing night as the Hammers lost 1-0 to a first-half goal and now faced an uphill battle in the return leg.

WEDNESDAY 15TH SEPTEMBER 1965

After losing 5-1 at home to Liverpool a week earlier, West Ham faced a daunting task in the return at Anfield. Geoff Hurst gave the Hammers a lead and although the Reds equalised through Geoff Strong – who was appearing as their first-ever substitute – 1-1 was creditable result.

SATURDAY 15TH SEPTEMBER 1979

Stuart Pearson scored his first goal for the club to seal a 2-0 victory over Sunderland at Upton Park. David Cross put West Ham ahead in a game which also saw debuts for Jimmy Neighbour and Ray Stewart.

TUESDAY 15TH SEPTEMBER 1992

The Hammers showed their desire for a quick promotion back to the First Division as they trounced Bristol City 5-1 at Ashton Gate. Mark Robson started the rout, scoring after six minutes, while Trevor Morley and Clive Allen each scored a brace.

SATURDAY 16TH SEPTEMBER 1961

There was plenty of drama at Upton Park in a very physical encounter with Chelsea. With no substitutes West Ham found themselves down to nine men! Phil Woosnam was already off the field being treated for injury, when keeper Lawrie Leslie was carried off after being kicked in the head. West Ham were leading 1-0 at the time after Geoff Hurst had scored in the sixth minute. Bobby Moore went in goal and the Hammers finally won 2-1 after Malcolm Musgrove netted the winner.

WEDNESDAY 16TH SEPTEMBER 1999

The Croatian side Osijek were the Hammers' first-ever opponents in the UEFA Cup. The tie, played at Upton Park before 24,331 fans, saw West Ham run out comfortable 3-0 winners. Scorers on the night were Paulo Wanchope, Paolo Di Canio and Frank Lampard.

SATURDAY 17TH SEPTEMBER 1960

Stanley Matthews graced the Upton Park pitch for the last time as Blackpool were the visitors for a First Division fixture. Languishing second to bottom in the league, the Seasiders played their part in a 3-3 draw. Full-back John Bond had given West Ham the lead and the other goals came from wingers Derek Woodley and Malcolm Musgrove.

WEDNESDAY 17TH SEPTEMBER 1975

West Ham travelled to Finland for their first-leg game in the European Cup Winners' Cup tie with Lahden Reipas as firm favourites, but the Finns shocked West Ham with a goal after just four minutes. The 4,587 spectators were pleased with their team's display as the game ended at 2-2. The Hammers' scorers were Trevor Brooking and Billy Bonds.

SATURDAY 17TH SEPTEMBER 1994

After six seasons with Everton, Tony Cottee returned to Upton Park. The Hammers were without a win so it was fitting that Cottee scored the late winner to give West Ham a 1-0 win over Aston Villa.

WEDNESDAY 18TH SEPTEMBER 1974

A home League Cup second round replay with Third Division Tranmere Rovers after the teams had drawn 0-0 at Prenton Park. On this occasion the Hammers romped home 6-0. Bobby Gould scored a hat-trick with Billy Bonds and Johnny Ayris completing the scoring.

WEDNESDAY 18TH SEPTEMBER 1996

The Hammers were shocked when Barnet took the lead in this second round first-leg League Cup tie at Underhill. In the second half Tony Cottee came to West Ham's rescue with an equaliser. In the Barnet side was Alan Pardew, who later became the West Ham manager.

SATURDAY 19TH SEPTEMBER 1959

Stamford Bridge was packed with a crowd of 54,349 for a First Division fixture between Chelsea and West Ham. The Hammers led 2-0 at the break with Malcolm Musgrove and Johnny Dick scoring. West Ham also scored twice, through Dick and Phil Woosnam, after the break to secure a 4-2 victory. Peter Brabrook and Jimmy Greaves featured for Chelsea, and both later joined West Ham.

SATURDAY 19th SEPTEMBER 1970

A disappointing 2-0 defeat to Newcastle United in front of 25,841 at Upton Park. Starring for the visitors was two-goal Pop Robson. Five months later he joined West Ham for a club record fee of £120,000.

TUESDAY 19th SEPTEMBER 1989

West Ham were at Birmingham City for the first-leg of their second round League Cup tie. The Hammers were leading through a goal from Martin Allen when the Blues equalised with four minutes remaining, but straight from the restart, Stuart Slater scored the winner to shock the home crowd of 10,987.

SATURDAY 20th SEPTEMBER 1919

In West Ham's inaugural Football League season, George Butcher and Syd Puddefoot score to secure a 2-1 home win over Rotherham County.

SATURDAY 20th SEPTEMBER 1980

Winger Bobby Barnes scored on his debut as the Hammers beat Watford 3-2 in an Upton Park thriller. Twice Watford were in front, but David Cross and Bobby Barnes levelled the scores. A minute from time Frank Lampard crossed for Trevor Brooking to head the winner.

SATURDAY 21st SEPTEMBER 1912

West Ham welcomed newly-promoted Merthyr Town to Upton Park for a Southern League match. Before 7,000 spectators, the teams drew 1-1 with Danny Shea scoring the Hammers' goal.

TUESDAY 21st SEPTEMBER 1966

A thriller at Eastville in the League Cup as West Ham drew 3-3 with Bristol Rovers in the second round. Two goals from Geoff Hurst and one from Johnny Byrne put the Hammers into a 3-1 lead after only 30 minutes. But a spirited show from Rovers saw them level the score.

SATURDAY 21st SEPTEMBER 1974

The Hammers went goal crazy in the space of three days. After beating Tranmere Rovers 6-0 a few days earlier, West Ham crushed Leicester City 6-2 at home on the Saturday. The goals flowed from Bobby Gould (two), Billy Jennings (two), Billy Bonds and Keith Robson.

SATURDAY 22ND SEPTEMBER 1981

First Division leaders West Ham continued their fine start to the season. Southampton were the visitors to Upton Park and were beaten 4-2 with Paul Goddard grabbing a hat-trick and Geoff Pike the other.

TUESDAY 22ND SEPTEMBER 1998

Popular full-back Julian Dicks made a courageous comeback having been out of the game for 18 months through injury. Playing at home to Northampton Town in the League Cup it took an injury-time goal from Frank Lampard to settle the tie.

SATURDAY 23RD SEPTEMBER 1911

Reading were Southern League Second Division champions when they came to play West Ham at Upton Park – but the Hammers were too good for the Berkshire team, beating them 5-0. There were five different scorers, each getting their first of the season: Frank Piercy, Tom Randall, Danny Shea, George Webb and Robert Whiteman.

SATURDAY 23RD SEPTEMBER 1961

The Hammers moved up to third in the First Division after a convincing 4-1 win at Sheffield United. Inside-forward Johnny Dick scored twice with further goals from Alan Sealey and Malcolm Musgrove. Three goals were scored in the last three minutes; the Blades scoring their goal with the very last kick of the match.

WEDNESDAY 23RD SEPTEMBER 1964

West Ham ventured into European competition for the first time when they travelled to Belgium to play La Gantoise. It was the first-leg of a second round European Cup Winners' Cup tie, and was played in front of a crowd of around 18,000. The only goal of the game was scored by Ronnie Boyce which gave West Ham a 1-0 advantage for the home leg.

SATURDAY 24TH SEPTEMBER 1938

Tranmere Rovers arrived at Upton Park for a Second Division game having lost all their previous away games. The Hammers added to their woes with a 6-1 hammering. Archie Macaulay netted a hat-trick, while Joe Cockroft and Norman Corbett scored their only goals of the season, and Joe Foxall completed the rout.

SATURDAY 24TH SEPTEMBER 1983

West Ham – top of the league – won their fourth successive home game by beating Notts County 3-0 at Upton Park. There were 20,613 to see goals from Trevor Brooking, Paul Goddard and a Ray Stewart penalty.

SATURDAY 25TH SEPTEMBER 1971

West Ham beat Stoke City 2-1. Clyde Best had scored in all three previous games and again he was on target in this match. Stoke drew level, but Bobby Moore got the winner with a looping shot.

TUESDAY 25TH SEPTEMBER 1984

West Ham were twice behind in a second round League Cup tie at Third Division Bristol City – but equalising goals from Tony Cottee and Steve Walford secured a 2-2 first-leg draw. The 15,894 crowd was the biggest gate of the season at Ashton Gate.

SATURDAY 26TH SEPTEMBER 1959

Ahead after a minute through Malcolm Musgrove, West Ham recorded a 4-1 win over West Bromwich Albion in the author's first-ever Upton Park match. Musgrove, Mike Grice and Phil Woosnam got the other goals.

MONDAY 26TH SEPTEMBER 1960

The Football League Cup was a new competition this season and the Hammers were at home to Charlton Athletic in round two. The game only drew an attendance of 12,496 but West Ham won 3-1 courtesy of goals from Johnny Dick, Bobby Moore and Malcolm Musgrove.

WEDNESDAY 26TH SEPTEMBER 1962

Having been knocked out of the FA Cup by Plymouth Argyle the previous season, the Hammers looked for revenge in the League Cup. They got it after Martin Peters scored in the third minute, followed by a Johnny Byrne hat-trick inside a 20-minute spell. Further goals followed from Malcolm Musgrove and Geoff Hurst to complete a 6-0 victory.

SATURDAY 27TH SEPTEMBER 1941

Centre-forward George Foreman was on form with a hat-trick in an 8-0 wartime win at Watford. Joe Foxall and Berry Nieuwenhuys each netted a brace with Sam Small getting the other goal.

SATURDAY 27TH SEPTEMBER 1969

West Ham had a tough time at Old Trafford, where despite two goals from Geoff Hurst they were beaten 5-2 by Manchester United. They were in the game until two United goals in the last ten minutes.

SATURDAY 28TH SEPTEMBER 1974

West Ham take their goal tally to 20 goals in four games as Burnley are beaten 5-3 at Turf Moor. In a remarkable game – even Trevor Brooking was booked – it was 1-1 at half-time. On target for West Ham were Keith Robson (two), Trevor Brooking, Billy Jennings and Billy Bonds.

SATURDAY 28TH SEPTEMBER 2002

A fierce London derby at Chelsea was won 3-2 by West Ham with Paolo Di Canio the star performer. After Jermain Defoe had cancelled out the Blues' early goal the Italian maestro took over with two wonderful goals. The first he juggled on his knee and then volleyed home from 25 yards.

MONDAY 29TH SEPTEMBER 1997

Losing 1-0 from the first-leg, West Ham played Huddersfield Town at Upton Park in the League Cup. The Yorkshiremen had no answer to the power of John Hartson who netted his first hat-trick in club football. The Hammers went through to the next round on a 3-1 aggregate score.

FRIDAY 29TH SEPTEMBER 2000

At an auction at Christies the 1966 England World Cup shirt belonging to Geoff Hurst was sold for a staggering £91,750.

SATURDAY 30TH SEPTEMBER 1950

A Second Division clash at Upton Park with Sheffield United produced eight goals. Leading scorer Bill Robinson scored his first-ever hat-trick putting West Ham in the lead three times. Unfortunately the Blades, aided by two own-goals from Ernest Devlin, came back to win 5-3.

THURSDAY 30TH SEPTEMBER 1999

A UEFA Cup tie in Croatia where the Hammers progressed to the next round after beating Osijek 3-1. After leading 3-0 from the first-leg, further goals from Paul Kitson, Neil Ruddock and Marc Vivien Foe put West Ham into the next round.

WEST HAM UNITED
On This Day

OCTOBER

WEDNESDAY 1st OCTOBER 1968

A third round replay at Highfield Road against Coventry City saw the Hammers knocked out of the League Cup. Goals from Geoff Hurst and Martin Peters were not enough as West Ham went down 3-2.

WEDNESDAY 1st OCTOBER 1975

Finns Lahden Reipas were at Upton Park for the second-leg of the European Cup Winners' Cup first round tie. Level from the first-leg, the Finns put up a good show by holding West Ham in the first half, but the Hammers were on top after the break as Pat Holland, Billy Jennings and Keith Robson scored in a comfortable 3-0 win.

WEDNESDAY 1st OCTOBER 1980

A bizarre night at Upton Park as the first-round second-leg Cup Winners Cup tie with Castilla was played behind closed doors – as a punishment for crowd trouble during the first-leg, which the Spanish side won 3-1. Initially West Ham were ordered to play 'home' European matches 300km away from Upton Park – Sunderland offered Roker Park as a venue. However, that decision was overturned. Instead the second-leg was played behind closed doors, in eerie atmosphere – each club was permitted a small delegation of staff and press and the official crowd was 262 – David Cross scored a hat-trick, and with Geoff Pike and Paul Goddard also on a target, a 5-1 win gave the Hammers a 6-4 aggregate win.

SATURDAY 2nd OCTOBER 1943

In the team for a wartime League South game against Crystal Palace at Selhurst Park were guest players Dai Jones of Leicester and Tommy Walker from Chelsea, as West Ham won 6-1 with goals from George Foreman (two), Joe Foxall (two), Jackie Wood and Len Goulden.

SATURDAY 2nd OCTOBER 1994

John Moncur scored his first West Ham goal: the winner in a 2-1 victory at Chelsea, after the home side had cancelled out Martin Allen's opener.

SATURDAY 3rd OCTOBER 1970

Burnley were the visitors and both teams were looking for a first win of the season. Making his debut was 17-year-old Johnny Ayris, who set up the first of three goals for Geoff Hurst, as West Ham were 3-1 winners.

SATURDAY 3RD OCTOBER 1981

West Ham maintained an unbeaten start to the season with a 2-2 draw at Birmingham City. David Cross twice gave the Hammers the lead; the Blues' second equaliser came a minute from time.

SATURDAY 3RD OCTOBER 1999

A fierce London derby against Arsenal at Upton Park saw referee Mike Reed dish out 12 yellow cards. He also sent off Marc Vivien Foe and Patrick Vieira. The Hammers won 2-1 thanks to the brilliance of Paolo Di Canio: he scored both goals. The first he lashed home from six yards but the second goal was sensational as he flicked the ball over Martin Keown with his left foot before clipping a 15-yard shot into the top corner with his right foot.

SATURDAY 4TH OCTOBER 1947

The day belonged to West Ham debutant Ken Tucker. The powerful winger scored a sensational hat-trick in the 4-0 home win over Chesterfield. George Proudlock claimed the other goal. Tucker did not score again for the club for four years!

SATURDAY 4TH OCTOBER 1958

Fresh from promotion, the Hammers were enjoying life as a First Division club and the home game with Blackburn Rovers brought a nine-goal thriller. Man of the match was centre-forward Vic Keeble who bagged four goals. West Ham won the game 6-3, with the other goals coming from Noel Cantwell and an own-goal.

WEDNESDAY 5TH OCTOBER 1966

There were 33,647 spectators at Highbury for a third round League Cup clash with Arsenal. A decent display from the Hammers saw them win 3-1 and progress to the fourth round, with two goals from Geoff Hurst and Martin Peters adding the other.

SATURDAY 5TH OCTOBER 1996

Mark Bowen featured for Wales against Holland in Cardiff. The World Cup qualifying match was won 3-1 by the Dutch. On the same day, Iain Dowie, Keith Rowland and Michael Hughes were in the Northern Ireland team that drew 1-1 with Armenia in Belfast.

TUESDAY 6TH OCTOBER 1987

A grim evening for the Hammers when they played at home to Barnsley in the League Cup second-round second-leg. Goalless from the first-leg, all was well when the Hammers raced into a two-goal lead with goals from Kevin Keen and Stewart Robson – but a complete collapse saw the Second Division side hit five to win the tie 5-2.

SATURDAY 6TH OCTOBER 1990

Steve Potts played in 399 league games but scored his goal in the home game with Hull City, as the Yorkshiremen were thrashed 7-1. Other scorers in the rout were Julian Dicks (two), Jimmy Quinn (two), George Parris and Trevor Morley.

WEDNESDAY 7TH OCTOBER 1964

European football was played at Upton Park for the first time as the Hammers welcomed La Gantoise, from Belgium, in the second-leg of their first round Cup Winners' Cup tie. West Ham won the first-leg 1-0. However, on this occasion they struggled, going a goal behind as Martin Peters scored an own-goal – but Johnny Byrne spared the blushes with a goal just before half-time for a 2-1 aggregate win.

SATURDAY 7TH OCTOBER 1967

West Ham were leading 3-0 at half-time in their home game with Stoke City, as Geoff Hurst scored twice and Martin Peters added another – but a second-half collapse saw the Potters score an amazing four goals in seven minutes to win 4-3.

SATURDAY 7TH OCTOBER 1978

The home game with Millwall was played in a hostile atmosphere: a helicopter hovered overhead during the game to spot any crowd trouble. On the pitch below, the Hammers put on a determined display – and Pop Robson rattled in a fine hat-trick in a 3-0 victory.

TUESDAY 8TH OCTOBER 1974

The Hammers faced a League Cup third round tie at Fulham. Skippering the home side was ex-Hammer Bobby Moore. Trevor Brooking gave West Ham a 1-0 lead but Fulham hit back to win 2-1. The Hammers avenged the defeat later that season in the FA Cup Final.

MONDAY 8th OCTOBER 1979

With no penalty shoot-outs in the seventies, West Ham faced a second replay to decide the third round League Cup tie with Southend. Played at Upton Park, the Shrimpers took the lead – but only kept it for two minutes as Billy Lansdowne equalised. The youngster then went on to grab a hat-trick. Further goals from Pat Holland and Ray Stewart gave the Hammers an emphatic 5-1 victory.

SATURDAY 9th OCTOBER 1965

West Ham – with the worst defensive record in the Football League – travelled to Nottingham Forest. In another poor display they were hammered 5-0 and slumped to 20th in the First Division. It was the Hammers' fourth five-goal drubbing in 12 games.

SATURDAY 9th OCTOBER 1982

The Hammers made it five successive wins by beating Liverpool 3-1 at Upton Park. Goals from Alvin Martin, Geoff Pike and Sandy Clark put West Ham in control before the Reds scored a late consolation goal.

TUESDAY 9th OCTOBER 1984

A League Cup second-round second-leg tie at home to Bristol City. After a 2-2 at Ashton Gate, the game was 1-1 at half-time – Tony Cottee scored West Ham's goal – but the visitors crumbled in the second half losing 6-1. Cottee added another goal with Paul Goddard scoring twice and there was one goal each from Steve Whitton and Steve Walford.

MONDAY 10th OCTOBER 1960

An Upton Park crowd of 12,496 watched the Hammers' first-ever League Cup tie against Charlton Athletic, which West Ham won 3-1 with strikes from Johnny Dick, Malcolm Musgrove and Bobby Moore.

SUNDAY 10th OCTOBER 1999

Making his full debut for England was Frank Lampard. He played in the 2-1 victory against Belgium at Sunderland's Stadium of Light.

TUESDAY 10th OCTOBER 2000

Michael Carrick was in the England under-21 team that drew 2-2 with Finland in the European Championship in Valkeakoski.

FRIDAY 10TH OCTOBER 2003

Jermain Defoe played in the England under-21 team that lost 1-0 to Turkey in Istanbul.

SATURDAY 11TH OCTOBER 1930

In a Division Two clash at Upton Park West Ham beat Manchester United 5-1. Claiming a hat-trick was Viv Gibbins with further goals from Jim Barrett and Jimmy Ruffell. The men from Old Trafford were relegated at the end of the season after finishing bottom.

SATURDAY 11TH OCTOBER 1986

A pulsating First Division game with Chelsea ended 5-3 to the Hammers before 26,859 at Upton Park. Frank McAvennie scored West Ham's first goal before Ray Stewart converted two penalties. With the score at 3-3, Tony Cottee was the hero scoring twice in the last five minutes.

SATURDAY 12TH OCTOBER 1957

West Ham were away to the league leaders Charlton Athletic in a Second Division fixture. In a terrific display the Hammers won 3-0. John Smith, Billy Dare and Malcolm Musgrove scored the goals – while goalkeeper Ernie Gregory saved a penalty.

SATURDAY 12TH OCTOBER 2002

Christian Dailly scored for Scotland during their 2-0 victory against Iceland in a European Championship game in Rejkjavic.

MONDAY 13TH OCTOBER 1890

Jack Mackesy was born in Deptford, south London. He gave good service to the club between 1911 and 1923 and played a total of 75 games for the club in the old Southern League, the Football League and in wartime football.

MONDAY 14TH OCTOBER 1957

A testimonial for long-serving Dick Walker against Sparta Rotterdam and a crowd of around 20,000 paid tribute to a great servant and also saw the debut of new signing Vic Keeble. He had joined from Newcastle. The game ended in a 5-0 victory, as Johnny Dick hit a hat-trick, Keeble got his first goal for the club and John Smith converted a penalty.

SATURDAY 14th OCTOBER 1989

Following two successive home defeats West Ham bounced back with a fine 2-0 win at league leaders Sheffield United. Winger Mark Ward netted both goals in a game which saw Julian Dicks miss a penalty.

SATURDAY 14th OCTOBER 2001

After losing 5-0 at Everton the previous week, the Hammers travelled to play Blackburn Rovers looking for a better display. On an afternoon of misery Tomas Repka was sent off and Rovers scored seven. For West Ham there was just the one goal – from Michael Carrick.

SATURDAY 15th OCTOBER 1977

The Hammers were bottom of the league when they played away to Wolverhampton Wanderers – but they went two up thanks to goals from Geoff Pike and Pop Robson and looked on course for only their second win of the season. However, Wolves fought back to draw 2-2.

TUESDAY 15th OCTOBER 2002

Both Joe Cole and Michael Carrick were in the England under-21 side that beat Macedonia 3-1 at Reading.

TUESDAY 16th OCTOBER 1962

A night to forget after a very poor showing from West Ham saw them slump to a disappointing 3-1 defeat at Second Division Rotherham United in the second round of the League Cup; Geoff Hurst was on target with the consolation goal.

WEDNESDAY 16th OCTOBER 1963

The Hammers faced Aston Villa at Villa Park in the second round of the League Cup in front of a crowd of 11,194. Second-half goals from John Bond and 17-year-old Martin Britt gave West Ham a 2-0 victory.

SATURDAY 16th OCTOBER 1965

For the home game with Sheffield Wednesday, the Hammers drafted 19-year-old centre-forward Martin Britt into the side. It was an inspired choice as the youngster responded with two fine goals in an excellent 4-2 victory. Martin Peters and John Sissons were the other scorers in front of a 20,690-strong crowd.

WEDNESDAY 16TH OCTOBER 2002

Steve Lomas was in the Northern Ireland team when they drew 0-0 with Ukraine in Belfast in a European Championship group match.

WEDNESDAY 17TH OCTOBER 1894

Centre-forward Syd Puddefoot was born in Bow, east London. He became a goalscoring legend at Upton Park with 28 goals in his 55 Southern League appearances. When the war broke out in 1914 he continued playing in the London Combination where he scored nearly a hundred goals in four seasons, including seven against Crystal Palace in 1918. He was transferred to Falkirk in 1922 where, in three years, he scored a further 45 goals for the Scottish club. In 1925 he returned south of the border to play for Blackburn Rovers, was capped three times by England and was a member of the Rovers' side that won the FA Cup in 1928. Syd came back to West Ham in 1931 for a couple of seasons before retiring as a player. He was later a coach in Turkey – to both Fenerbahce and Galatasaray – before becoming the manager at Northampton Town in 1937. He died in 1972 after contracting pneumonia.

SATURDAY 17TH OCTOBER 1970

A new record attendance of 42,322 was set at Upton Park for the visit of Tottenham Hotspur. Centre-half Tommy Taylor made his debut after signing from Orient for £170,000. Peter Eustace and Geoff Hurst were the Hammers' scorers in a 2-2 draw.

WEDNESDAY 18TH OCTOBER 1989

A great night for the Hammers as they humble Sunderland 5-0 at Upton Park. It was one way traffic all the way as Martin Allen scored after eight minutes followed by goals from Stuart Slater and Kevin Keen making it 3-0 at half-time. A further two stunning goals came late in the game from 22-year-old Eamonn Dolan.

SATURDAY 19TH OCTOBER 1958

The Hammers were enjoying their first season in the top flight. Playing away at West Bromwich Albion, they fell behind on 21 minutes but Vic Keeble equalised on the hour mark. West Ham looked like they had done enough for a decent away point, but the Albion were awarded a penalty with six minutes remaining which was converted for a 2-1 win.

MARTIN ALLEN

SATURDAY 19TH OCTOBER 1968

Hapless Sunderland were thrashed 8-0 at Upton Park with World Cup hero Geoff Hurst claiming six goals – a record breaking hat-trick in each half. Bobby Moore and Trevor Brooking were the other scorers before an attendance of 24,718 – ironically the lowest of the season.

SATURDAY 19TH OCTOBER 1985

Aston Villa were at Upton Park and took the lead on six minutes. The partnership between Tony Cottee and Frank McAvennie was flourishing as they continued their rich vein of form. Both netted twice in a 4-1 win, while nine players were booked, six from Villa.

WEDNESDAY 20TH OCTOBER 1971

A League Cup replay at Elland Road, after Leeds United had forced a 0-0 draw at Upton Park. It was still 0-0 after 90 minutes, but in extra-time Clyde Best headed home a cross from Harry Redknapp to put the Hammers into the fourth round.

SATURDAY 20TH OCTOBER 1984

After losing heavily the previous week at Old Trafford, the Hammers were looking to bounce back at bottom club Stoke City, and the Potters handed West Ham a goal start with an own-goal. Paul Allen, Tony Cottee and Paul Goddard added further goals as the Hammers recorded a 4-2 win.

SATURDAY 21ST OCTOBER 1911

A home Southern League game with Brentford saw an amazing scoreline, as for a second time in the season, the Hammers won 7-4! Three players in the game scored hat-tricks: Bill Kennedy and Danny Shea for West Ham and Willis Rippon for the Bees. The other Hammers' goal was credited to Fred Harrison.

SATURDAY 21ST OCTOBER 1972

A seven-goal bonanza at Maine Road as Manchester City beat the Hammers 4-3. Six of the goals came in the first half, with Clyde Best and Johnny Ayris scoring for West Ham, who trailed 4-2 at the break. A rare headed goal from Bobby Moore in the second half gave West Ham hope of a draw but it was not to be.

WEDNESDAY 21st OCTOBER 1999

A poor night for West Ham as they slumped to a 2-0 defeat in Romania against Steaua Bucharest in the first-leg of a second-round UEFA Cup tie played before a small crowd of 12,500.

SATURDAY 22nd OCTOBER 1955

A disappointing attendance of just 13,303 saw the Hammers beat Doncaster Rovers 6-1 at Upton Park. Those who stayed away missed a a thriller with Harry Hooper claiming a hat-trick. Other scorers were Jimmy Andrews, Billy Dare and Ken Tucker.

SATURDAY 22nd OCTOBER 1960

A fine career start for 17-year-old Ronnie Boyce as he made his debut in the home game against Preston North End. Malcolm Musgrove netted a hat trick in a fine 5-2 victory, while a penalty from John Bond and a Johnny Dick goal added to the score.

WEDNESDAY 22nd OCTOBER 1980

Playing at home in the European Cup Winners' Cup the Hammers brushed aside the threat of Romanians Poli Timisoara. Two goals within the space of a minute from Billy Bonds and Paul Goddard set West Ham on their way. David Cross scored another and Ray Stewart scored a penalty to complete a fine 4-0 victory.

SATURDAY 23rd OCTOBER 1937

Goalkeeper Brian Rhodes was born in Marylebone, London. He made his Hammers debut in September 1957 against Blackburn Rovers and went on to play a total of 66 league and cup matches. In 1963 he joined Southend United but played in only 11 games for the Third Division side. He then emigrated to Australia where he was coach to the Australian Olympic squad. Brian tragically died in 1993 when he lost a battle against leukaemia.

WEDNESDAY 23rd OCTOBER 1996

A League Cup third round tie against Nottingham Forest at Upton Park. Hugo Porfirio – on loan from Sporting Lisbon – gave a dazzling display in the 4-1 win, setting up two goals for Iain Dowie and scoring himself. The fourth goal was a penalty scored by Julian Dicks.

SATURDAY 24TH OCTOBER 1925

The Hammers were undefeated in their first five games – but had been on a downward spiral ever since, and the trip to West Bromwich Albion was a disaster. Winger Jimmy Ruffell scored for West Ham but Albion replied with a seven-goal blast to win 7-1.

MONDAY 24TH OCTOBER 1960

The first season of the League Cup saw West Ham away to Fourth Division Darlington, where they suffered the first of many giant-killing acts the Hammers have had to endure over the years. The Quakers scored in the first minute and West Ham slumped to a 3-2 defeat. Dave Dunmore and Johnny Dick goals were not enough to avoid embarrassment.

SATURDAY 25TH OCTOBER 1975

The top-of-the-table clash with Manchester United attracted a gate of 38,528 to Upton Park. Alan Taylor gave West Ham the lead on six minutes but the Reds equalised in the second half just after the game had been held up due to trouble on the terraces. With 20 minutes left Bobby Gould snatched the winner, converting a cross from Graham Paddon.

WEDNESDAY 25TH OCTOBER 1983

A sparse crowd of 10,896 was inside Upton Park for the visit of Bury in the League Cup – but those fans present witnessed the biggest win in the club's history. The Fourth Division Shakers were completely outclassed as the rampant Hammers won 10-0. West Ham scored the first goal after just two minutes. Tony Cottee led the way with four goals – three of them were headers – and there were two-goal hauls for both Trevor Brooking and Alan Devonshire. Alvin Martin and Ray Stewart netted one apiece to take the total to double figures.

SATURDAY 26TH OCTOBER 1940

A wartime home league game with Southend United attracted a crowd of around 5,000 to Upton Park. The luckless Shrimpers had already taken two seven-goal beatings from Arsenal that season and in this match things did not get any better for them. West Ham won with ease, hammering the Essex club 11-0. There were six different goalscorers: George Foreman hit four, while Joe Foxall got a hat-trick. Jim Barrett, Len Goulden, Archie Macaulay and Ted Fenton all got one goal each.

MONDAY 26TH OCTOBER 1959

In the 1950s West Ham played in the Southern Floodlight Cup, which was regarded as a first team competition. Playing at home to Reading, centre-forward Harry Obeney grabbed four goals in a 6-1 victory. Joining in the goal spree were Andy Smillie and Mike Grice.

WEDNESDAY 27TH OCTOBER 1971

The visit of Liverpool in the League Cup drew a massive crowd of 40,878. The Reds went into the lead after half an hour. West Ham hit back with a goal from Geoff Hurst and then Pop Robson netted a late winner for a 2-1 victory.

SATURDAY 27TH OCTOBER 1984

Arsenal came to Upton Park having won their last five games and were shocked when West Ham took a 2-0 lead through Tony Cottee and Paul Goddard. The Gunners reduced the deficit but West Ham wrapped up the points when grabbing a third from Geoff Pike for a 3-1 victory.

SATURDAY 28TH OCTOBER 1972

West Ham were undefeated at home at this stage in the 1972/73 season and the run continued against bottom club Crystal Palace. Bobby Moore set up two goals for Trevor Brooking in the first half, before John McDowell scored his first goal for the club after the break. Pop Robson added a fourth to complete an emphatic 4-0 victory.

SATURDAY 28TH OCTOBER 1978

The Hammers were favourites to win the Second Division and there were 32,634 packed inside the Goldstone Ground for the clash with fellow promotion chasers Brighton & Hove Albion. On-form Pop Robson scored first for the Hammers but the Albion equalised six minutes before the interval. The Seagulls were only level for four minutes, as Robson scored again and West Ham held on for a 2-1 victory.

SATURDAY 29TH OCTOBER 1932

Both Burnley and West Ham had been scoring and conceding plenty of goals in the early part of the season, so there was little surprise when the sides drew 4-4 at Upton Park. Legendary scorer Vic Watson got a hat-trick with another goal coming from winger John Morton.

TUESDAY 30TH OCTOBER 1934

The Irish capital Dublin was the birthplace of goalkeeper Noel Dwyer. He signed for West Ham from Wolverhampton Wanderers in 1958, having made just five appearances for the Midlands side. He played in a total of 36 league games for West Ham before being transferred to Swansea Town in 1960. He was capped 36 times by the Republic of Ireland and later had spells at Plymouth Argyle and Charlton Athletic. Noel sadly died in 1992.

SATURDAY 30TH OCTOBER 1971

Undefeated in seven matches, the Hammers travelled to south London to face Crystal Palace. Making a dream debut was 17-year-old Nigerian Ade Coker who scored after seven minutes. Further goals followed from Billy Bonds and Clyde Best to give West Ham a deserved 3-0 win.

SATURDAY 30TH OCTOBER 1982

After two First Division defeats on the south coast, at Brighton and Southampton, West Ham bounced back by beating Manchester United 3-1 at home. Roared on by an Upton Park crowd of 31,684, the Hammers built up a three-goal lead through Paul Goddard, Ray Stewart and Geoff Pike. United scored a consolation goal in the last minute of the game.

MONDAY 31ST OCTOBER 1977

An England XI was invited to provide the opposition for Trevor Brooking's testimonial match. A crowd of 23,220 turned out to pay tribute to the West Ham star, and saw the Hammers win 6-2. Fittingly Brooking scored the first goal, Derek Hales scored a hat-trick and Geoff Pike and Pop Robson also notched one apiece. Hammers legend Geoff Hurst had hung up his boots, but the crowd were delighted to see him make an appearance as a second-half substitute for West Ham.

SATURDAY 31ST OCTOBER 1998

Playing away to Newcastle United the score was 0-0 at half-time, but early in the second half Newcastle full-back Stuart Pearce – who later joined West Ham – was sent off. The Hammers took control with Ian Wright grabbing two goals and Trevor Sinclair adding another for a good 3-0 win at St James's Park.

WEST HAM UNITED
On This Day

NOVEMBER

SATURDAY 1st NOVEMBER 1913

A good day for leading scorer Dick Leafe who, in an away game at Coventry City, notched his first hat-trick for the club. Albert Denyer was the other scorer in a fine 4-2 win.

SATURDAY 1st NOVEMBER 1975

The Hammers were second in the First Division and in confident mood as they travelled to Birmingham City, but went a goal down after five minutes. However, inspired by Trevor Brooking, who scored the equaliser, West Ham fought back to win 5-1. Alan Taylor netted two with further goals coming from Frank Lampard and an own-goal.

TUESDAY 1st NOVEMBER 1988

Derby County were the visitors for a fourth round League Cup tie. Struggling in the league, West Ham hit form with a 5-0 win. Alvin Martin (two), Ray Stewart, Leroy Rosenior and Kevin Keen got the goals.

SATURDAY 2nd NOVEMBER 1968

A treat for the 36,008 crowd as London rivals Queens Park Rangers were beaten 4-3 at Upton Park. World Cup heroes Bobby Moore, Martin Peters and Geoff Hurst gave the Hammers a 3-1 lead but the best goal of the game was scored by Harry Redknapp, volleying a late winner.

TUESDAY 2nd NOVEMBER 1976

Fulham were the opposition for Frank Lampard's testimonial. Playing in the Cottagers' side were Bobby Moore and George Best. Fulham took the lead, but goals from Keith Robson, Trevor Brooking and Lampard gave the Hammers a 3-1 win before a crowd of 16,597.

SATURDAY 3rd NOVEMBER 1945

A Football League South match against Southampton at Upton Park ended in a 3-1 win for the Hammers. Centre-forward Sammy Small scored a hat-trick. His marker was the future England boss Alf Ramsey.

WEDNESDAY 3rd NOVEMBER 1965

The Hammers faced a tough League Cup test at Rotherham who were undefeated at home in Division Two – but goals from Geoff Hurst and Bobby Moore saw West Ham win 2-1 and progress to Round Five.

SATURDAY 3RD NOVEMBER 1992

Trevor Morley came to West Ham's rescue as he volleyed an equaliser against Grimsby Town in a 1-1 draw which kept the Hammers in fourth spot in the First Division.

SATURDAY 4TH NOVEMBER 1961

A thriller at Maine Road as Peter Dobing scored a first half hat-trick to put Manchester City in firm control – Johnny Dick also netted once for the Hammers before the break. The second half saw a complete turnaround as West Ham rattled in four goals: another from Dick, two from Alan Sealey, and Malcolm Musgrove added the fifth in the last minute to make the score 5-3. Seconds from time, Bobby Moore was sent off for the only time in his career following a foul.

WEDNESDAY 4TH NOVEMBER 1999

A disappointing night in east London as the Hammers bowed out of the UEFA Cup. Playing against Steaua Bucharest the Hammers were 2-0 down from the first-leg, and despite being on top throughout, they couldn't breach the Romanians' defence and the tie ended 0-0.

SATURDAY 5TH NOVEMBER 1960

The fireworks were early at Upton Park as Welsh wizard Phil Woosnam had the game of his life as he inspired West Ham to a 6-0 home win over Arsenal. The Gunners were outplayed with Dave Dunmore scoring a hat-trick. There were also goals from Johnny Dick and Woosnam, plus a rare strike from Andy Malcolm.

SATURDAY 5TH NOVEMBER 1966

After losing at Fulham the previous month the Hammers got revenge when at Upton Park with a 6-1 win. Geoff Hurst rammed in four goals with England colleague Martin Peters adding two.

WEDNESDAY 5TH NOVEMBER 1975

A European night in east London as West Ham met Ararat Erevan, from Russia, in the Cup Winners' Cup. Tied at 1-1 from the first-leg, the Hammers progressed to the next round by virtue of a 3-1 win. There were 30,399 to see goals from Graham Paddon, Keith Robson and Alan Taylor.

SATURDAY 6TH NOVEMBER 1976

Tottenham Hotspur and West Ham were at the foot of the table when they met at Upton Park. With both defences giving away goals it was an eight-goal thriller for the fans. The Hammers came out on top, winning 5-3 with five different goalscorers. Finding the net were Pop Robson, Billy Bonds, Trevor Brooking, Billy Jennings and Alan Curbishley. Spurs never recovered and were relegated that season.

WEDNESDAY 6TH NOVEMBER 2002

Old boys Iain Dowie and assistant David Cross brought their Oldham team to Upton Park for a third round League Cup tie. It was a Hammers horror show as the Second Division team progressed with a 1-0 win.

SATURDAY 7TH NOVEMBER 1931

A home game with West Bromwich Albion: to be remembered for an outstanding goalscoring feat. Unfortunately for Hammers' fans it was Billy Richardson, the Albion centre-forward, who scored an amazing four goals in five minutes during the Baggies' 5-1 win. The Hammers' lone goal came from Jimmy Ruffell.

SATURDAY 7TH NOVEMBER 1953

Inside-forward Johnny Dick scored the first hat-trick of his career as Bury were demolished 5-0 at home. Dave Sexton and Roy Stroud were also on target in this Second Division match.

MONDAY 7TH NOVEMBER 1966

This home fourth-round tie with Leeds United saw one of the finest displays West Ham have produced in the League Cup. The Leeds team was packed with international players but inspired by the brilliance of Johnny Byrne, who was involved in five of the goals, the magnificent Hammers crushed them 7-0. Geoff Hurst and Johnny Sissons scored hat-tricks with Martin Peters grabbing the other goal.

TUESDAY 8TH NOVEMBER 1983

West Ham were at home to Brighton & Hove Albion for their 100th League Cup tie. They celebrated by winning 1-0 courtesy of a goal from Dave Swindlehurst which put the Hammers through to the fourth round of the competition.

SATURDAY 8TH NOVEMBER 2003

A home game to savour. West Bromwich Albion were the visitors, and Jermain Defoe scored in the opening minute. Brian Deane added two more to give the Hammers a 3-0 lead after 18 minutes – but disaster struck as Albion hit back with four goals – two in either half – to win 4-3. To make matters worse, Defoe was sent off just before half-time.

SATURDAY 9TH NOVEMBER 1963

Highbury was the setting for the London derby with Arsenal. Johnny Byrne netted after 12 seconds to give the Hammers a dream start, but the Gunners came back and twice took the lead. Byrne added another to equalise and Martin Peters got the final goal in the thrilling 3-3 draw.

WEDNESDAY 9TH NOVEMBER 1988

The Simod Cup game with West Bromwich Albion attracted just 5,960 hardy spectators to Upton Park. It was a personal triumph for Leroy Rosenior who scored four goals in a 5-2 win, David Kelly got the other.

SATURDAY 9TH NOVEMBER 1996

In a World Cup qualifying match in Eindhoven, Mark Bowen was in the Welsh team beaten 7-1 by Holland.

SATURDAY 10TH NOVEMBER 1990

A red hot derby at The Den against fierce rivals Millwall. With 20,598 inside the ground creating a hostile atmosphere, the Lions went ahead just after half-time – but with 15 minutes left Frank McAvennie equalised for a 1-1 draw, much to the delight of the Hammers contingent.

SATURDAY 10TH NOVEMBER 2001

A memorable day for Hammer Trevor Sinclair, who won his first-ever England cap in the 1-1 draw against Sweden at Old Trafford.

SATURDAY 10TH NOVEMBER 2007

The Hammers recorded their biggest win of the 2007/08 season as they tore Derby County apart at Pride Park, thrashing the hapless Rams 5-0. Lee Bowyer scored a brace, Matty Etherington also scored and an own-goal added to the gloom for the home side – but the best of the bunch was a stunning strike from Nolberto Solano.

SATURDAY 11TH NOVEMBER 1944

Another wartime game with a bizarre score line. With Upton Park out of action due to bomb damage the Hammers were playing their 12th away game of the campaign at Fulham. West Ham won the game 7-4 with five of the goals coming from guest players. Jock Dodds, from Sheffield United, scored a hat-trick and George Ludford, from Tottenham, scored twice. Len Goulden and Ted Fenton completed the scoring.

SATURDAY 11TH NOVEMBER 1995

Alvin Martin was granted two testimonials, the second against Chelsea. An entertaining game ended 3-3 with goals from Tony Cottee, Marco Boogers and Danny Williamson. Guesting in the West Ham line-up were Liverpool pair Steve McManaman and Jamie Redknapp.

SATURDAY 12TH NOVEMBER 1966

One of the best London derbies seen in years was the verdict on the Hammers' 4-3 triumph over Tottenham at White Hart Lane. It was magical stuff for the 57,157 fans who saw the Hammers take a 3-1 lead through Peter Brabrook, Johnny Byrne and John Sissons. Jimmy Greaves missed a penalty for Spurs, but they still came back to level at 3-3 – but with 13 minutes left, Hurst headed a winner.

SATURDAY 12TH NOVEMBER 1983

When the teams met at Molineux the Wolves had gone 18 games without a win and were bottom of the league. Second-placed West Ham won 3-0. Dave Swindlehurst scored his ninth of the season with Tony Cottee and Trevor Brooking adding one each.

SATURDAY 12TH NOVEMBER 1988

Despite two goals from David Kelly the Hammers went in at half-time losing 3-2 at home to Nottingham Forest. After the interval Leroy Rosenior came to the rescue, earning a point with a diving header.

SATURDAY 13TH NOVEMBER 1926

There was a sparse attendance of 7,647 at Upton Park for the visit of Aston Villa. Those who did turn up were rewarded with a 5-1 victory with Vic Watson claiming a hat-trick. Stan Earle and Tommy Yews completed the scoring.

MONDAY 13th NOVEMBER 1972

Manchester United provided the opposition for the Ronnie Boyce testimonial game. There were 19,247 to see the Hammers win 5-2. Dudley Tyler and Pop Robson both scored twice with Trevor Brooking scoring the fifth.

SATURDAY 14th NOVEMBER 1942

Spectators watching wartime regional games usually saw plenty of goals. This game was no exception, as the 5,000 who were present for the home game with Millwall were rewarded with 12 goals. The Hammers were winning 6-1 at half-time but the Lions came back to score four goals in the second half, with the game ending 7-5. Those on the scoresheet were Len Goulden (three), Richard Dunn (two) with one each from George Foreman and Joe Foxall.

SATURDAY 14th NOVEMBER 1970

Two goals from Clyde Best and an effort from Bobby Moore put West Ham into a 3-1 lead against Wolverhampton Wanderers – but the visitors stunned the home crowd with two goals in the last seven minutes to draw level at 3-3.

WEDNESDAY 14th NOVEMBER 1973

In a friendly at Wembley Stadium England lost 1-0 to Italy. It was Bobby Moore's 108th and last international.

SATURDAY 15th NOVEMBER 1997

Rio Ferdinand won his first cap when he came on as a substitute for England in their friendly game at Wembley against Cameroon.

SATURDAY 15th NOVEMBER 2003

In a European championship match in Glasgow, Scotland beat Holland 1-0. Winning his 50th cap for Scotland was Christian Dailly.

MONDAY 16th NOVEMBER 1970

Bobby Moore's testimonial match against Celtic was played in a fiercely competitive spirit. There were around 11,000 Celtic fans in attendance and they saw their side take the lead three times, but Geoff Hurst, John Ayris and Clyde Best all hit levellers for the Hammers.

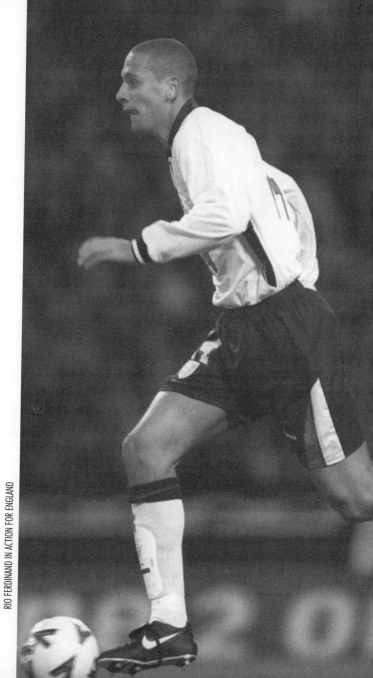

WEDNESDAY 16TH NOVEMBER 1977

England beat Italy 2-0 in a World Cup qualifier at Wembley. Trevor Brooking played a prominent part in the first goal and scored the second.

MONDAY 17TH NOVEMBER 1958

The Malcolm Allison testimonial game attracted an attendance of 21,600 where the Hammers played an All Star XI. It was fantastic entertainment with West Ham winning 7-6. In the All Star team were Brian Clough and Bobby Charlton. The referee was Jimmy Hill with two Irish linesmen, namely Frank O'Farrell and Danny Blanchflower.

WEDNESDAY 17TH NOVEMBER 1971

A perfect hat-trick from Pop Robson helped West Ham beat Sheffield United 5-0 in the League Cup at Upton Park. He scored one goal with his head, another with his right foot and the other with his left. Clyde Best got the other two goals.

SATURDAY 18TH NOVEMBER 1967

West Ham lost at home for the sixth time in a row as Manchester City won 3-2 at Upton Park. Young full-back Frank Lampard made his debut but the defeat left the Hammers with the worst home record in all four divisions. Geoff Hurst and Martin Peters were on target with the two West Ham goals.

SATURDAY 18TH NOVEMBER 1995

A good all-round performance as West Ham comfortably beat Bolton Wanderers 3-0 at Burnden Park. All the goals came in the second half, from Ian Bishop, Tony Cottee and Danny Williamson – who ran some 80 yards from his own area with the ball before scoring.

WEDNESDAY 18TH NOVEMBER 1999

Both Rio Ferdinand and Ian Wright were in the England team that beat the Czech Republic 2-0 at Wembley in a friendly.

TUESDAY 19TH NOVEMBER 1997

Walsall were at Upton Park for a League Cup tie. A smartly-taken hat-trick from Frank Lampard and a goal from John Hartson saw the Hammers win 4-1 and progress to the fifth round.

MONDAY 19th NOVEMBER 2001

A goal feast for the fans as the Hammers drew 4-4 with Charlton Athletic at The Valley. Paul Kitson, who had not played for almost two years, was drafted into the side and promptly scored a hat-trick. Jermain Defoe, who had signed from Charlton, scored the other goal.

SATURDAY 20th NOVEMBER 1965

The Hammers were beaten by Arsenal for the first time in 32 years. The First Division match at Highbury saw Geoff Hurst and Martin Peters score but the Gunners ran out 3-2 winners.

SATURDAY 20th NOVEMBER 1993

Headed goals from Alvin Martin and Trevor Morley gave West Ham a 2-0 home win against Oldham Athletic. The Latics were down to ten men in the second half following a sending-off.

SATURDAY 21st NOVEMBER 1959

Football League Champions Wolverhampton Wanderers provided tough opposition at Upton Park, but the Hammers raced into a 3-0 lead thanks to a Johnny Dick hat-trick. Wolves came back strongly with two second-half goals but West Ham held on to win 3-2.

SATURDAY 21st NOVEMBER 1981

The home game with Coventry City was delayed for 20 minutes due to floodlight failure at Upton Park – but the break in play didn't unsettle the Hammers who were in good form and won comfortably 5-2. Alvin Martin scored twice within the space of five minutes, Ray Stewart converted a penalty kick and two further strikes came from Trevor Brooking and Jimmy Neighbour.

SUNDAY 21st NOVEMBER 1999

The Premiership game with Sheffield Wednesday was a Sunday thriller at Upton Park. Paulo Wanchope put the Hammers ahead, but they found themselves losing 2-1. Marc Vivien Foe equalised, but the Hammers conceded again to trail 3-2. Enter Paolo Di Canio, playing against his old club, who levelled the scores from a penalty. And there were huge scenes of delight when Frank Lampard hit a screamer to give West Ham a 4-3 win.

SATURDAY 22ND NOVEMBER 1919

It was West Ham's first season in the Football League and they faced a Second Division encounter with Fulham. They won 2-0 with both goals scored by centre-forward Syd Puddefoot.

SATURDAY 22ND NOVEMBER 1958

West Ham boasted an impressive home record, having lost just once in eight games – but lowly Leicester City were the visitors and provided the First Division's shock of the day. They scored three first half goals and held on to win 3-0.

TUESDAY 23RD NOVEMBER 1971

An all-star European XI provided the opposition for the Geoff Hurst testimonial match. In the European team were Eusebio, Uwe Seeler, Jimmy Greaves and Rodney Marsh. Geoff Hurst scored for West Ham, but the European team led 4-1 with 15 minutes remaining. However, the Hammers fought back with two goals from Pop Robson and one from Clyde Best to draw 4-4, much to the delight of the 29,250 crowd.

SATURDAY 23RD NOVEMBER 1985

The Hammers were fourth in the First Division, winning games, and Frank McAvennie was scoring plenty of goals. There was no change at Coventry City as West Ham won for the sixth successive match. McAvennie scored the only goal of the game.

WEDNESDAY 24TH NOVEMBER 1965

Competing in the European Cup Winners' Cup as the holders, West Ham beat Olympiakos 4-0 in the second round home first-leg. Geoff Hurst scored twice, with one each from Peter Brabrook and Johnny Byrne.

TUESDAY 24TH NOVEMBER 1992

Clive Allen hit two goals as the Hammers beat Reggiana at home in the Anglo-Italian Cup. Trevor Morley was sent off in the first half.

WEDNESDAY 25TH NOVEMBER 1964

Czech Cup winners Sparta Prague were at Upton Park for the first-leg of a second round tie in the Cup Winners Cup. West Ham won 2-0 with two second half goals from John Bond and Alan Sealey.

SATURDAY 25TH NOVEMBER 1989

A Second Division clash with Blackburn Rovers deserved a bigger attendance than the 10,238 fans who turned up at Ewood Park. Despite a goal from Liam Brady, West Ham were losing 5-1 just after half-time but they almost made a great comeback. Goals from Julian Dicks, Stuart Slater and Mark Ward gave the Hammers some hope but they ran out of time and the game ended in a 5-4 defeat.

SATURDAY 26TH NOVEMBER 1932

Performing poorly away, the Hammers were scoring freely at home. Playing Charlton Athletic at Upton Park the scoring spree continued with a 7-3 win. Vic Watson and Arthur Wilson each scored a brace, with one apiece for Jim Barrett, John Morton and Tommy Yews.

TUESDAY 26TH NOVEMBER 1991

A home Zenith Data Systems Cup with Brighton & Hove Albion drew a crowd of 8,146. A 2-0 victory – with both goals coming from Frank McAvennie – put West Ham into the southern section semi-final.

SATURDAY 27TH NOVEMBER 1976

Despite being bottom of the First Division the Hammers won away for the first time in a year, beating Manchester United 2-0 at Old Trafford. Trevor Brooking and Billy Jennings secured the win with first-half goals.

SATURDAY 27TH NOVEMBER 1999

Trevor Sinclair pounced seconds before half-time to score against Liverpool at Upton Park. It was Sinclair's fourth goal of the season and the 1-0 win moved West Ham up to ninth in the Premiership.

MONDAY 27TH NOVEMBER 2000

Rio Ferdinand was transferred from West Ham to Leeds United for a British record transfer fee of £18million.

SATURDAY 28TH NOVEMBER 1981

An away match at Leeds United saw the Hammers trailing 3-1 in the second half – Trevor Brooking had scored West Ham's goal. David Cross added a second to reduce the deficit, before Brooking grabbed the equaliser to make it 3-3 with four minutes left to play.

SATURDAY 28TH NOVEMBER 1998

West Ham won for the third successive Premiership match by beating Tottenham Hotspur 2-1 at home. The win took the Hammers into the dizzy heights of second spot. The star man was tricky winger Trevor Sinclair who scored both goals.

WEDNESDAY 29TH NOVEMBER 1989

A meagre crowd of 5,409 at Upton Park were cheered by five Hammers goals. Playing against Plymouth Argyle in the Zenith Data Systems Cup, there were five different scorers in the 5-2 win: Kevin Keen, Eamonn Dolan, Julian Dicks, Alvin Martin and Stuart Slater.

THURSDAY 29TH NOVEMBER 2001

West Ham's Paolo Di Canio won the FIFA Fair Play award for 2001 after catching a cross and spurning an easy goal-scoring attempt at Everton because their goalkeeper was lying injured.

TUESDAY 30TH NOVEMBER 2010

West Ham beat the holders and league leaders Manchester United 4-0 in the Carling Cup quarter-final at Upton Park. Two goals each for Jonathan Spector and Carlton Cole thrilled the 33,551 spectators.

WEDNESDAY 30TH NOVEMBER 1988

A great night at Upton Park as Liverpool were beaten 4-1 in a League Cup fourth round tie. It was the Reds' biggest post-war cup defeat. Star of the night was young midfielder Paul Ince – a future Liverpool player – who scored two cracking goals. Tony Gale and an own-goal completed the scoring on a night of celebration in east London.

TUESDAY 30TH NOVEMBER 1999

A thrilling end to the League Cup tie at Birmingham City saw the Hammers progress to the next round. Steve Lomas had scored in the first half, but with three minutes remaining West Ham were losing 2-1. Then up stepped Paul Kitson for the equaliser in the 87th minute, and two minutes later, Joe Cole, scoring his first goal for the club, hit a late winner to secure a 3-2 win and a place in round five.

WEST HAM UNITED
On This Day

DECEMBER

WEDNESDAY 1st DECEMBER 1937

Playing for England against Czechoslovakia at White Hart Lane were both John Morton and Len Goulden. Morton was one of the scorers in England's 5-4 victory.

WEDNESDAY 1st DECEMBER 1965

The Hammers were in Greece to play Olympiakos in the second-round second-leg tie in the European Cup Winners' Cup. Leading 4-0 from the match in London, Martin Peters scored twice to give West Ham a huge lead. The Greeks came back to level the game at 2-2 but it was the Hammers who easily progressed to the next round.

SATURDAY 2nd DECEMBER 1978

Second Division Cambridge United made their first-ever visit to Upton Park and found themselves a goal down after three minutes as Tommy Taylor scored for the Hammers. Pop Robson scored with 20 minutes remaining and Cambridge conceded a further three goals to lose 5-0. Robson was on target for his second with Billy Bonds and Alan Curbishley completing the rout.

TUESDAY 2nd DECEMBER 1980

Second Division West Ham beat their old rivals Tottenham Hotspur 1-0 in a League Cup fifth round tie at Upton Park. A tense affair was settled nine minutes from full-time when David Cross headed home Trevor Brooking's cross.

TUESDAY 3rd DECEMBER 1912

The village of Wombwell, in Yorkshire, was the birthplace of winger Stan Burton. He first joined Doncaster Rovers and was then transferred to Wolverhampton Wanderers in 1938. He was a regular in the Wolves side in 1938-39, making 32 appearances, and played for them in the 1939 FA Cup Final. In a strange transfer he then joined West Ham and became the first player in history to appear in a cup final and then play for another club before the end of the season. He was in the team that defeated Manchester City 2-1 in May and that was his only official appearance for the club. He did play in three league games the following season but, due to the outbreak of war, the league was abandoned and the games deleted from the records.

SATURDAY 3RD DECEMBER 1960

In driving rain at Upton Park West Ham defeated newly-promoted Cardiff City 2-0. Malcolm Musgrove scored from a Johnny Dick pass; the second came when Dave Dunmore slotted home.

SATURDAY 3RD DECEMBER 1988

Fierce rivals Millwall were unbeaten at The Den prior to playing the Hammers, but a goal after 17 minutes from Paul Ince was enough to give West Ham a 1-0 victory. The Hammers' fans were escorted from the ground at the end by a huge police presence.

WEDNESDAY 4TH DECEMBER 1991

Carrow Road was the venue for a League Cup tie with Norwich City. Mike Small equalised in the second half, after Norwich had taken a first-half lead, but the Hammers' hopes were dashed when City scored the winner from the penalty spot a minute from the end.

SATURDAY 4TH DECEMBER 2004

It was a good victory for West Ham as they won away at promotion rivals Sunderland. A second-half goal from Marlon Harewood and a last-minute goal from Teddy Sheringham gave the Hammers a 2-0 win.

SATURDAY 5TH DECEMBER 1964

West Ham had scored in every league game that season until they played at home to Leicester City. The first man to stop the Hammers scoring was goalkeeper Gordon Banks, who pulled off some amazing saves during a 0-0 draw. He was saved by the woodwork on two occasions though, as both Johnny Byrne and John Sissons hit the bar.

SATURDAY 5TH DECEMBER 1970

The Hammers were 19th in the table when they travelled to play Derby County, and needed a good performance. Jimmy Greaves, playing in his 500th league game, scored the Hammers' first goal. Trevor Brooking added another and Clyde Best scored twice to clinch a 4-2 victory.

WEDNESDAY 6TH DECEMBER 1967

Both Bobby Moore and Geoff Hurst were in the England team that drew 2-2 with Russia in a friendly at Wembley.

TUESDAY 6th DECEMBER 1983

It took Everton two attempts to knock West Ham out of the League Cup fourth round. After a 2-2 draw the Hammers went to Goodison Park for a replay. Goalless at full-time, the Blues won 2-0 in extra-time.

SATURDAY 7th DECEMBER 1957

A top-of-the-table clash with Liverpool at Anfield in the Second Division finished 1-1 extending West Ham's impressive unbeaten run to ten games. Johnny Dick scored for the seventh successive match.

TUESDAY 7th DECEMBER 1982

A cracking game at Meadow Lane as the Hammers and Notts County draw 3-3 in the League Cup fourth round. Twice County went ahead but François Van Der Elst equalised. He scored a third to make it 3-2, but County levelled with two minutes to play.

SATURDAY 8th DECEMBER 1951

The Hammers had only lost one home game all season prior to Sheffield Wednesday's visit, but the Owls were in brilliant form and won this game 6-0 with their centre-forward Derek Dooley scoring a hat-trick.

WEDNESDAY 8th DECEMBER 1992

On a waterlogged pitch in Italy the Hammers beat Cosenza 1-0 in the Anglo-Italian Cup. A Clive Allen volley clinched the win before an attendance of just 800 who braved the diabolical conditions.

SATURDAY 8th DECEMBER 2001

A classic eight-man move finished with a goal from Jermain Defoe and gave West Ham a 1-0 win away to Manchester United, making it two wins in two seasons at Old Trafford.

SATURDAY 9th DECEMBER 1961

Popular Czech goalkeeper Ludek Miklosko was born in Ostrava. He joined West Ham in 1990 and went on to play a total of 365 League and Cup games. For a transfer fee of £266,000 he proved to be a tremendous bargain. He left in 1998 to end his playing career at Queens Park Rangers. Miklosko came back to West Ham in 2001 to be the goalkeeping coach – a role he still enjoys today.

WEDNESDAY 9TH DECEMBER 1964

Before a crowd of 45,000 in Prague, the Hammers lost 2-1 to Sparta Prague in the Cup Winners' Cup. Johnny Sissons had given the Hammers the lead but two late goals were conceded. However, West Ham progressed to the third round by virtue of their 2-0 first-leg win.

SATURDAY 10TH DECEMBER 1960

The Tyneside faithful were treated to an amazing ten-goal thriller as West Ham drew 5-5 away to Newcastle United. Malcolm Musgrove, Dave Dunmore, John Bond, Johnny Dick and an own-goal had given the Hammers a 5-2 lead with only 11 minutes remaining. Then came a collapse as the Geordies came back to level the scores.

WEDNESDAY 10TH DECEMBER 1975

Trailing 1-0 from the first-leg in Italy, West Ham were hoping to overturn the deficit when they played host to Fiorentina in the Anglo-Italian Cup. Unfortunately the Italians scored after 20 minutes and held on defensively for the remainder of the game to win 1-0.

SATURDAY 11TH DECEMBER 1999

The third round FA Cup ties were brought forward to December. The Hammers were drawn away to Tranmere Rovers. A first-half goal gave Tranmere a 1-0 win and they were added to the list of lower-division clubs who have knocked West Ham out of cup competitions.

WEDNESDAY 11TH DECEMBER 2002

The Slovakian full-back Vladimir Labant returned home after a one-year stay at Upton Park. He was signed from Sparta Prague for £900,000 but he only played in 12 Premiership games and two FA Cup ties.

WEDNESDAY 12TH DECEMBER 1979

Second Division West Ham were playing their ninth League Cup tie of the season against Nottingham Forest. The teams had drawn 0-0 at Upton Park, but Forest won the replay 3-0 in extra-time.

SATURDAY 12TH DECEMBER 1992

For the fourth successive week Clive Allen and Trevor Morley scored. Both got headers as Southend United were beaten 2-0 at Upton Park.

SATURDAY 13TH DECEMBER 1958

A forgettable debut for young right-back Joe Kirkup at Maine Road. He was on the losing side as Manchester City – aided by a hat-trick from Colin Barlow – won 3-1. Johnny Dick scored for the Hammers.

SATURDAY 13TH DECEMBER 1997

An Upton Park encounter with Sheffield Wednesday who fielded their Italian star Paolo Di Canio. The Hammers won 1-0 with a strike from Paul Kitson. It was the fifth consecutive home win.

SATURDAY 14TH DECEMBER 1985

The Hammers march on and were now undefeated in 17 First Division games. Goals from Frank McAvennie and a penalty from Ray Stewart gave them a 2-0 home victory over Birmingham City. They were now in third spot in the table, behind leaders Liverpool only on goal difference.

SATURDAY 14TH DECEMBER 1996

In Belfast, Northern Ireland beat Albania 2-0 in a World Cup qualifying match. Michael Hughes played, while Iain Dowie scored both goals.

SATURDAY 15TH DECEMBER 1951

A good day for West Ham's new centre-forward Bert Hawkins. Playing against Queens Park Rangers at Upton Park he scored a hat-trick in a 4-2 victory. Terry Woodgate got the other before a 17,549 crowd.

WEDNESDAY 15TH DECEMBER 1965

Third Division Grimsby Town were at Upton Park for a fourth round League Cup replay. Having drawn 2-2 initially, West Ham won 1-0. Geoff Hurst scored, maintaining a record of scoring in every round.

WEDNESDAY 15TH DECEMBER 1982

Alvin Martin was in the England team that beat Luxembourg 9-0 at Wembley in a European Championship qualifying game.

WEDNESDAY 16TH DECEMBER 1963

West Ham thumped Fourth Division Workington 6-0 in a fifth round League Cup tie. The crowd of 10,160 saw Johnny Byrne (three), Ron Boyce, Geoff Hurst and Tony Scott get the goals.

SATURDAY 16TH DECEMBER 2000

West Ham extended their unbeaten run in the Premiership to eight matches after drawing 1-1 against Everton at Goodison Park. Fredi Kanoute scored the equalising goal with seven minutes remaining.

SATURDAY 17TH DECEMBER 1960

Third-placed Wolves were comprehensively beaten 5-0 at Upton Park. Bobby Moore scored his first goal for the club with other goals coming from Dave Dunmore (two), Johnny Dick and Malcolm Musgrove.

SATURDAY 17TH DECEMBER 1966

Chelsea and West Ham served up a ten-goal spectacular at Stamford Bridge. The Hammers led 2-0 and 5-3. But Chelsea fought back to make it 5-5 with the last kick of the match. The Hammers scorers were John Sissons (two), Peter Brabrook, Johnny Byrne and Martin Peters.

SATURDAY 17TH DECEMBER 1994

The Hammers won their first Premiership game in eight when they beat Manchester City at home 3-0. It was a personal triumph for Tony Cottee who grabbed a hat-trick.

SATURDAY 18TH DECEMBER 1993

A thrashing in Yorkshire for the Hammers as they lost 5-0 to Sheffield Wednesday. They had no answer to former England winger Chris Waddle who made three goals and scored one himself.

WEDNESDAY 18TH DECEMBER 1996

On a rain-soaked pitch Stockport County dumped West Ham out of the League Cup in a replay at Edgeley Park. Julian Dicks gave the Hammers the lead but County respond with two goals to clinch the tie 2-1. It was a bad night for Iain Dowie who first headed an own-goal and then added to his personal woes when he broke his ankle.

TUESDAY 19TH DECEMBER 1989

An exciting Zenith Data Systems Cup tie at Stamford Bridge saw West Ham beaten 4-3. A small crowd of 8,408 saw Chelsea take a 2-0 lead. West Ham hit back with three goals from Kevin Keen, Stuart Slater and David Kelly. The Blues equalised before netting an injury-time winner.

WEDNESDAY 19TH DECEMBER 1990

West Ham were away to Luton Town in the Zenith Data Systems Cup It was a poor display on the plastic pitch and the Hammers were beaten 5-1. Kevin Keen netted the goal, following up on a saved penalty.

THURSDAY 19TH DECEMBER 1996

West Ham signed Mike Newell on loan from Birmingham City. He went on to make six starts and one substitute appearance but never scored a goal. Mike was a journeyman of football having played for 11 different clubs in his career.

SATURDAY 20TH DECEMBER 1958

Bottom club Portsmouth were crushed 6-0 at home in the First Division. Phil Woosnam scored his first Hammers goal followed by strikes from Vic Keeble (two), Johnny Dick, Malcolm Musgrove and John Smith.

MONDAY 20TH DECEMBER 1965

The first-leg of the League Cup semi-final brought Cardiff City to Upton Park. Despite two late goals from the Welshmen the Hammers ran out 5-2 winners. There were five different scorers; namely Bovington, Brabrook, Byrne, Hurst and Sissons.

SATURDAY 20TH DECEMBER 1969

Against rivals Tottenham at White Hart Lane, West Ham won 2-0 with goals from Martin Peters and Geoff Hurst. It was the Hammers' first away win for nine months. Jimmy Greaves missed a Spurs penalty.

SATURDAY 21ST DECEMBER 1974

West Ham extended their unbeaten run in the First Division to eight matches as they drew 1-1 with Chelsea at Stamford Bridge. Bobby Gould volleyed the Hammers' equaliser with five minutes remaining.

TUESDAY 21ST DECEMBER 1982

The Fourth Round League Cup replay with Notts County at home saw the Hammers pull off a routine 3-0 win. It was an easy night's work – and West Ham also had two goals disallowed before opening the scoring with a penalty from Ray Stewart. Further goals were added in the second half, from Sandy Clark and Paul Allen.

FRIDAY 22ND DECEMBER 1950

Newcastle was the birthplace for centre-half Bill Green. He signed for West Ham in 1976 for £100,000 from Carlisle United. He played for two seasons making 40 appearances before being transferred to Peterborough United in 1978. Bill later played for Chesterfield and Doncaster Rovers.

SATURDAY 22ND DECEMBER 1962

Some superb pre-Christmas entertainment for a crowd of 44,650 at White Hart Lane. Tottenham Hotspur were winning 2-0, but the Hammers turned the deficit into a 4-3 lead with goals from Joe Kirkup, Ron Boyce, Martin Peters and Tony Scott. In the dying minutes Dave Mackay completed a hat trick to level the scores at 4-4.

MONDAY 22ND DECEMBER 1997

The experienced French goalkeeper Bernard Lama was signed on loan from Paris St Germain. A class act, he played in 14 games enhancing his reputation and was chosen for the 1998 World Cup squad. At the end of the season he returned to the Paris giants.

SATURDAY 23RD DECEMBER 1933

Centre-forward Vic Watson scored his 15th goal of the season in the 5-3 home win against Notts County in the Second Division. Winger Jimmy Ruffell scored a brace with John Morton and Len Goulden joining in with one goal each.

SATURDAY 23RD DECEMBER 1995

A bad day at the Riverside Stadium as the Hammers suffered the first of five successive away defeats. Middlesbrough, inspired by Brazilian playmaker Juninho, were leading 3-0 after half an hour. Tony Cottee and Julian Dicks replied to give the score a more respectable look but Boro scored again to win the game 4-2.

SATURDAY 24TH DECEMBER 1955

After three successive home defeats West Ham returned to winning ways by beating Swansea Town 5-1 at Upton Park. The five different scorers were John Bond, Johnny Dick, Billy Dare, Harry Hooper and Ken Tucker.

SATURDAY 24TH DECEMBER 1960

A tough game for West Ham as they were away to Tottenham Hotspur who had lost only once all season. Therefore it was no surprise that Spurs came out on top, winning 2-0.

SATURDAY 25TH DECEMBER 1915

A wartime London Combination game with Arsenal attracted 5,500 to Upton Park for a morning kick-off. The Hammers were lucky to be able to call on the services of local hero Syd Puddefoot who scored five goals. The game finished with West Ham having won 8-2, with further goals from Bill Masterman (two) and Danny Shea.

THURSDAY 25TH DECEMBER 1958

The last-ever game to be played on a Christmas Day at Upton Park saw the visitors being old rivals Tottenham Hotspur. Second-half goals from Vic Keeble and Johnny Dick gave the First Division Hammers a 2-1 win before 26,178 spectators.

THURSDAY 26TH DECEMBER 1963

Inspired by Bryan Douglas, league-leaders Blackburn Rovers gave West Ham a lesson in finishing. Johnny Byrne scored twice for the Hammers but it was the Rovers who scored eight to win 8-2. It was their biggest-ever away victory.

FRIDAY 26TH DECEMBER 1980

A shock for league-leaders West Ham when they travelled to play Queens Park Rangers, as they were beaten 3-0. However, after this game the Hammers didn't lose again in the league that season.

TUESDAY 26TH DECEMBER 2000

A Boxing Day pounding for Alan Curbishley's side as Charlton Athletic were beaten 5-0 in the Premiership at Upton Park. An own-goal from Richard Rufus started the rout, followed by strikes from Fredi Kanoute (two), Frank Lampard and Trevor Sinclair.

MONDAY 27TH DECEMBER 1948

Centre-forward Ken Wright scored twice as the Hammers won 3-2 against Leeds United at Elland Road. Johnny Dick was the other scorer.

SATURDAY 28th DECEMBER 1957

West Ham were in fine form and looking a good bet to be promoted to the First Division. In another good display Bristol Rovers were beaten 6-1 at home. Johnny Smith, aged just 18, claimed his first hat-trick with Vic Keeble scoring twice and a further goal from Johnny Dick.

SATURDAY 28th DECEMBER 1963

Having lost 8-2 at home to Blackburn Rovers on Boxing Day West Ham faced them again at Ewood Park. In a remarkable transformation, they won 3-1 with goals from Johnny Byrne (two) and Geoff Hurst.

SATURDAY 29th DECEMBER 1962

On a snow-covered pitch at Nottingham Forest and trailing 3-1, a superb late rally saw two goals from Peter Brabrook and one from Johnny Byrne turn the game into a 4-3 victory. The first goal was an own-goal.

SATURDAY 29th DECEMBER 2001

Trevor Sinclair opened the scoring for West Ham, before England striker Michael Owen equalised in a 1-1 draw with Liverpool.

SATURDAY 30th DECEMBER 1967

Brian Dear had scored a hat-trick against Leicester on Boxing Day and then followed this with two more at Filbert Street in a fine 4-2 win, which also saw Trevor Brooking and John Sissons on the scoresheet.

SATURDAY 30th DECEMBER 1978

Blackburn Rovers were beaten 4-0 on a bitter afternoon at Upton Park. Trevor Brooking set up three of the goals for David Cross, Pop Robson and Alan Taylor. The final goal was an own-goal.

SATURDAY 31st DECEMBER 1966

England goalkeeper Gordon Banks became the first keeper to keep a clean sheet against West Ham in 1966/67. He had a superb game and Leicester snatched a goal to win 1-0.

SATURDAY 31st DECEMBER 1994

Ian Bishop, Tony Cottee and Michael Hughes all scored in a 3-1 Premiership win over Nottingham Forest at Upton Park.

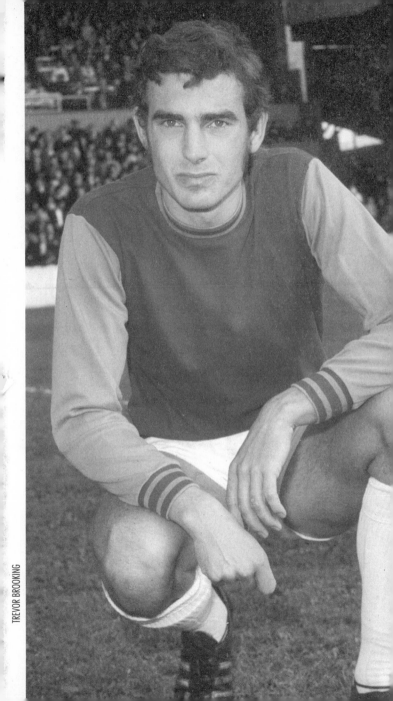